Birds of the Yare Valley:
a site guide

David Bryant

Birds of the Yare Valley: a site guide

Published by
Heathland Books

For further copies of this book, please e-mail
info@spacerocksuk.com
Telephone 01603 715933

Designed and typeset by Bob Tibbitts (iSET)
Printed in Great Britain

Foreword
by Dr Rob Bryant

MY one and only younger brother has been passionate about wildlife as long as I've known him, which is now getting on for seventy years.

We were both keen to explore every aspect of the world about us from a very early age. Our parents hardly needed to encourage us, but, by taking us on holidays all over Britain, they expanded what would otherwise have been a relatively narrow horizon. We were introduced to the wildlife of Devon and Cornwall, Wales and the Highlands of Scotland well before we left Primary School.

A little later in life, when I lived in Anglesey for 18 months, the birds and plants of this fabulous place rekindled an interest in the natural world that remains undiminished. Once David had become a little older, he also rediscovered his childhood passions. I wasn't surprised, therefore, that when he qualified as a teacher in 1972, David took his cue from the birds and migrated to Norfolk!

David never does anything by halves and became a serious twitcher during the 1980s-1990s. I barely make the grade as a birder, but am irrationally pleased that I have a bird on my list (Golden-winged Warbler) that he's unlikely to add to his, despite his warp-speed drive down the A12 to a housing estate in Maidstone, Kent!

Nowadays we take great pleasure in 'gripping each other off' with photos of birds we've taken on our travels. Just like old times during our childhood travels in a Dormobile: nothing wrong with a little healthy sibling rivalry!

I'm pleased that he finally got around to writing an account of his favourite stamping ground, the Yare Valley. He probably knows as much about its wildlife as anyone and his ability to describe it in an entertaining way should give this book pride of place on any birder's bookshelf.

Rob Bryant, June 2017

Introduction

AT just over eighty kilometres in length, the Yare is one of the major rivers of Norfolk. Rising west of Shipdham, it flows eastwards through Barnham Broom, Bawburgh, Colney and Norwich before its confluence with the River Wensum at Whitlingham. Now larger and more strongly tidal, the Yare meanders towards the coast, passing the villages of Bramerton, Brundall, Rockland St Mary and Cantley. Along its course it is connected by dykes or sluices to a number of medieval peat diggings, long flooded to form the Yare Broads. Although less-well visited than the Northern Broads of the rivers Bure, Thurne and Ant, for hundreds of years these have been acknowledged for the richness and variety of their flora and fauna.

At Hardley Cross the smaller River Chet adds its waters as the Yare passes through the remote pastures and reed swamps of the Halvergate and Berney Marshes. A few miles inland of the North Sea the Yare joins the Waveney to form the tidal Breydon Water: from here the River Yare passes under Breydon and Vauxhall bridges, joining the River Bure to complete the short journey to the sea at Gorleston.

Following the last ice age the Breydon estuary was much more extensive and the coastline of the North Sea reached as far inland as Acle and Bramerton. Vast amounts of water from melting glaciers trapped behind the Cromer-Holt ridge flowed southwards from North Norfolk, producing the wide river valleys we see today. Looking from Mill Hill, Strumpshaw, it's possible to imagine the prehistoric River Yare stretching to the high ground of the southern horizon.

For anyone who enjoys walking in the countryside or who has an interest in wildlife, the Yare Valley has a lot to offer along its entire length. It's one of the few places in eastern England where it is possible to walk all day and meet only the occasional cow or sheep: additionally, given the valley's range of different habitats, it's one of the best regions to encounter local or nationally scarce species such as Bittern, Bearded Tit, Swallowtail Butterfly and Norfolk Hawker dragonfly.

Of course nothing is forever and during the nearly fifty years I've enjoyed watching – and latterly photographing – the plants and animals of the Yare Valley there have been many changes: some for the better, some for the worse. A major problem for the whole region has been water abstraction: large areas of what were once marsh and reedswamp are now under the plough or are grazed by sheep and cattle. Back in 1975 I caught an eighteen pound Pike from Tunstall Dyke where it ran under the A47 by the old landmark Stracey Arms pub. This waterway once carried wherries and barges from the River Bure to Halvergate: now it is a trickle just a few centimetres deep. As a result of this lowering of the water table, the sight of thousands of geese and swans over-wintering on the marshes is becoming less predictable and breeding species such as Redshank, Oystercatcher and Bittern are seemingly in decline. Fortunately, large areas of the Yare Valley are now set aside as nature reserves, under the protection of the Norfolk Wildlife Trust and the Royal Society for the Protection of Birds and, in theory, future prospects look increasingly bright. These reserves are not by any means the only places to encounter wildlife – nor even the best – but they certainly have the potential to provide havens from which, hopefully, animals and plants can spread out to re-establish themselves in other suitable locations.

As far as I have been able to discover, there isn't an up-to-date book that aims to tell the reader exactly what birds (and other interesting wildlife) can be found in the Yare Valley throughout the year, and, more importantly perhaps, exactly where they can be found. This book is intended to fill this gap and will be regularly revised as the situation demands. Of course, where the locations of sensitive or especially protected species are known, these won't be included, merely an acknowledgement that they do occur in the region.

Most of the photographs in this book are mine: needless to say (given my long-standing interest in the more unusual species) these include rare or hard-to-see birds such as Common Crane, Glossy Ibis, Twite and so on.

However, this book is not primarily intended as a rare bird guide.

For those of you who enjoy a spot of twitching, online websites and Twitter feeds provide daily records of any really rare migrants that have been discovered: their URLs are listed in an appendix. Rather, the book is intended as a reference to glance through before a visit to the region and to take out with you once you've arrived! Having said which, it would seem redundant to list every common species at every site, so these will be referred to in group terms, such as 'the usual woodland species'. I have included references to many of the rarer birds that have turned up in recent years, just to add that frisson of excitement to your visit! Every part of the Yare Valley from Marlingford to Gorleston is covered by this guide which attempts to provide details of exactly *what* you can see, *when* you can see it and *where* you can park! The sketch maps are not totally to scale, but show major routes and sites of wildlife interest.

Although the majority of the species covered by the book are birds, most of us welcome the chance to see unusual plants, insects and mammals. Where such opportunities exist at the locations described, they are included in the text.

Catching up with many of the species highlighted in this book frequently requires a bit of a walk: to help plan your visit, I've included distances or rough timings wherever possible, as well as descriptions of the conditions you might encounter: the riverside paths at Strumpshaw Fen, for example, can resemble a first world war battlefield in the winter: wellies definitely required!

Being a river, the Yare has two banks! The birding sites to the *south* of the river can only be reached by driving out of Norwich on the A146 Beccles Road and then north on one of the many country lanes that service the communities along the river valley. The sites on the *north* side of the valley to the east of Norwich are reached from the A47 southern by-pass that ultimately leads to Great Yarmouth. For convenience, sites on the south of the valley are headed in blue, those on the north side in **black**.

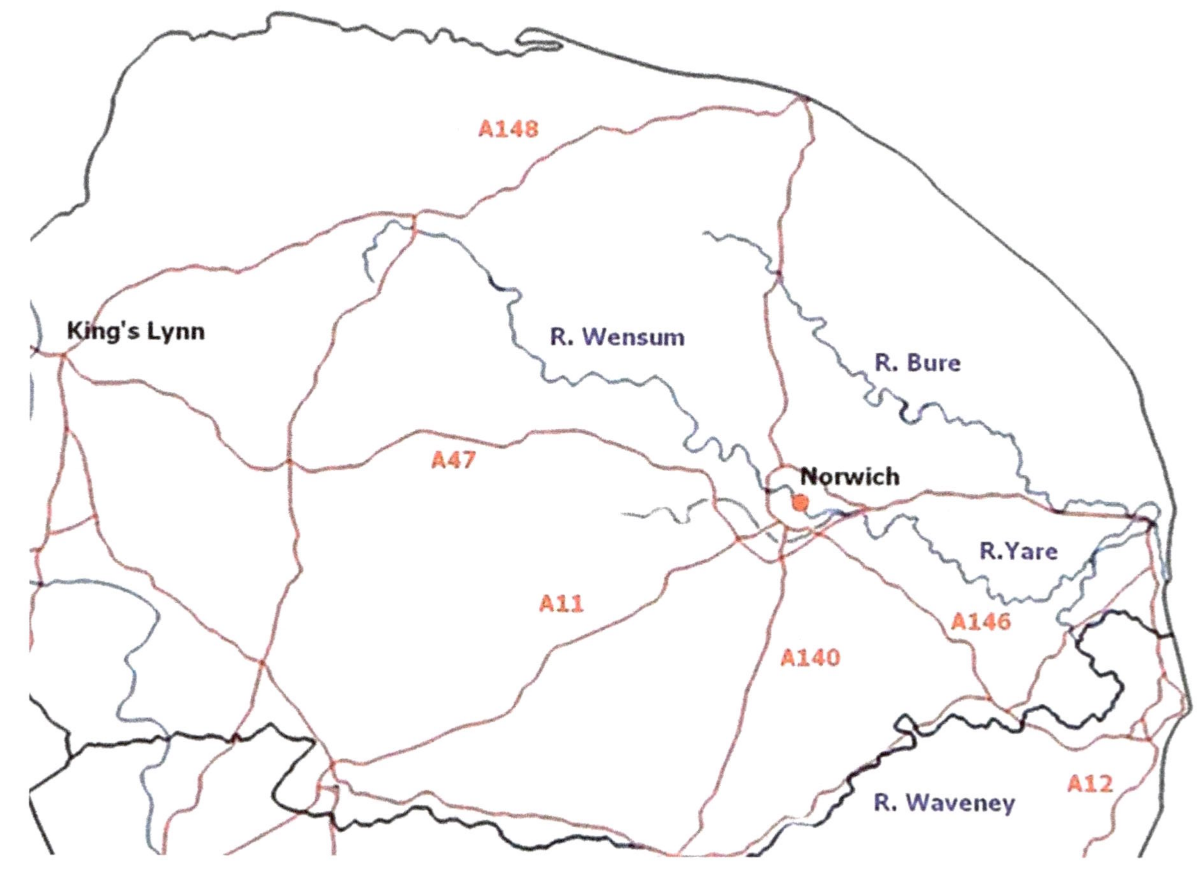

A148
King's Lynn
R. Wensum
R. Bure
A47
Norwich
R.Yare
A11
A146
A140
A12
R. Waveney

Contents

Buzzards are a widespread breeding species in East Norfolk

Once a rare bird of mid-Wales, Kites now breed in the Yare Valley

The Upper Yare Valley: Marlingford to Eaton

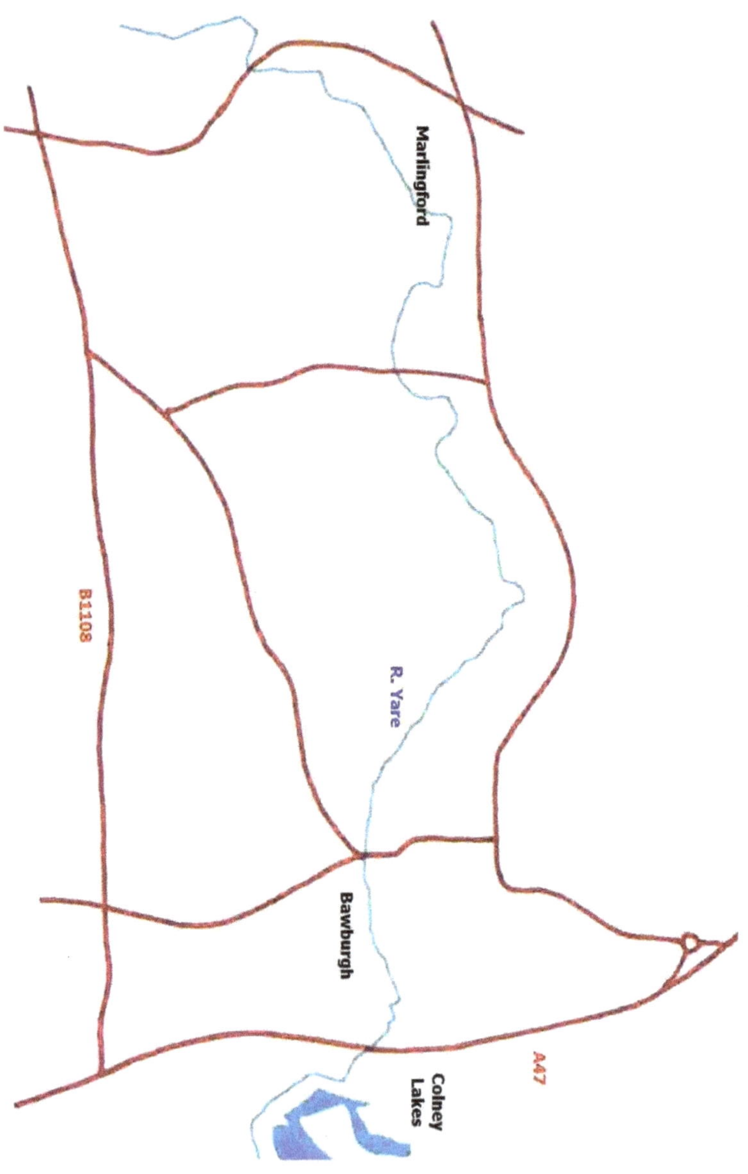

The Upper Yare Valley: Marlingford to Eaton

FOR the first few kilometres of its journey from its source at Shipdham to the western outskirts of Norwich, the Yare meanders through agricultural land, grazing marsh and alongside syndicated fishing waters: the large complex of lakes at Barford, for example, includes stretches of the River Yare and River Tiffey, and the whole area attracts an excellent variety of birds at all seasons. Here, as elsewhere in these upper reaches, casual access is often difficult or unobtainable.

Marlingford Mill

With its picturesque mill pool and leats, this is the first location in the Yare Valley of interest to birders. Even here, parking is at a premium and access patchy: at the time of writing there is room for a few cars in front of the mill itself and for a few more along the roadside.

The Yare (more of a stream than a river at this point!) looks good for Grey Wagtails, and indeed, as is increasingly the case with many suitable upper reaches of Norfolk's rivers, these delightful birds can be encountered here at all seasons. One cannot but wonder whether Dippers will also colonise these fast-flowing stretches in the future: certainly Norfolk is increasingly visited by the continental Black-bellied race. Predictably, Kingfishers can be seen fishing in the mill pool or back-eddies: more often, however an almost subliminal flash of blue is a more typical view. The trees alongside the Yare downstream of the mill hold all the usual woodland suspects, while the grazing meadows have produced Great White Egret and American Wigeon in the past. Getting a decent view of either was to say the least problematical and involved peering through hedges or finding a field gate to park in! Red

Kites and Common Buzzards are frequently seen soaring over the shallow valley: both species are regular and increasing breeders in the region.

To drive to Marlingford, head west on the A47 southern ring road until you see signs for the Norfolk Showground. Take the slip road and then the first left on the roundabout: follow the road as it bends right towards Marlingford. (The water meadows on the left have held Great Egret on several occasions) Turn left into Mill Road at the Marlingford Bell PH: the Mill is on the right after about half a kilometre.

Postcode: NR9 5HW

Bawburgh Mill

The mill pool is another regular site for Grey Wagtails and Kingfishers and has hosted Black-bellied Dippers several times: on one occasion two individuals were present. Follow the directions above for Marlingford, but turn left into Harts Lane to Bawburgh.

Postcode: NR9 3LS

Bawburgh Lakes

This angling complex east of the A47 at Colney offers very limited numbers of bird watching permits: these can be applied for via their website. There is a large heronry at the site, as well as variable numbers of Tawny, Little and Barn Owls. The Lakes are occasionally visited by Ospreys and Black Terns on passage and a few pairs of Common Terns breed. Kingfishers are regular and are frequently seen whirring over the water. In the winter various species of wildfowl drop in: these occasionally include Goosander, Goldeneye and Scaup. In 2015 a Lesser Scaup was reported, but never conclusively identified. Great (White) Egret and Purple Heron have both been recorded and Little Egrets are frequently encountered here and on the grazing marshes nearby.

Bowthorpe Marshes

Sadly under continual threat from developers, this delightful open expanse of meadow, marsh and scrub is criss-crossed by paths that allow excellent views of the Yare and of numerous shallow pools. A Great Egret (or perhaps two) has over-wintered here for a number of years: although it moves up and down the valley, this has generally been one of the best places in East Norfolk to catch up with the species. Cormorants are often seen drying their wings perched in the riverside trees, while Buzzards and Red Kites soar overhead. The scrub along the northern edge of the marsh holds Linnets, Goldfinches and all the expected warblers, thrushes and garden species. In recent years, this suburb of Norwich has hosted long-staying winter flocks of Waxwing. Access by walking south from the small car park along Chapel Break Road, Bowthorpe.

Postcode: NR5 9HY

Earlham Park

Situated just to the east of the Yare, this is a popular location for dog walkers and families. Nevertheless, it throws up some surprises at times, including Yellow-browed Warbler on several recent occasions. It's not unusual to see a Kingfisher flash past along the river, but generally the best chance would be in the winter when fewer paddlers and dog walkers are around.

Postcode: NR4 7TQ

University of East Anglia Broad

Despite the name, this deep, tree-lined water is not strictly a broad, since it was created by gravel extraction during the building of the University. Possibly because of the number of birding undergraduates and environmental science students who watch the area as a 'home patch', some surprising birds have been recorded. Although there is naturally some disturbance from anglers and UEA students, there are always Great Crested Grebes, Mute Swans and other water birds present, while the gull flock hosted a Ring-billed Gull – Norfolk's first record of the species – in 1991. The winter is generally the most productive period for wildfowl, and Pintail, Goldeneye and Goosander are fairly regular. To access the Broad, park at the pitch and putt car park on South Park Avenue, walk along the edge of the golf course, cross over Bluebell Road then take the path through the hedge. The path continues across meadows to the end of the broad.

Postcode: NR4 7ED

Grey Wagtail at Marlingford Mill

Bohemian Waxwing, Bowthorpe

Treecreeper in an Alder at Marlingford Mill

Kingfishers are a regular sight throughout the Yare Valley

Bluebell Marsh

The River Yare runs just west of the UEA Broad and there is a permissive footpath along its northern bank that leads to the A11 flyover: some parking is available off the Eaton Road. This can be a good site for woodland and meadow species such as Treecreeper, Green and Great Spotted Woodpecker and the usual tits and warblers, while Kingfishers are frequently encountered along the river.

Eaton Park

Despite being a popular recreational amenity with a café and an occasional venue for open air music concerts, the Park holds a reasonable population of woodland species, including Treecreeper, Nuthatch and the expected summer warblers.

Postcode: NR4 7AU

Birds of the upper Yare

Spring:

As is frequently the case, the Yare seems to be used by migrating birds as an aid to navigation: in the spring almost anything on the British list can turn up, but the various gravel pits and fishing lakes (if you can obtain permission to visit) may host pairs of Little Ringed Plovers and are visited annually by an Osprey or two. Black and Arctic Terns are seen on passage most years, often just ahead of a thunder storm!

Summer:

Common Tern, Blackcap, Whitethroat, Lesser Whitethroat, Willow Warbler, Chiffchaff. Reed Warbler, Sedge Warbler, Grasshopper Warbler.

Autumn

As with Spring passage, migrating species often drop into the upper Yare valley for a day or two.

Winter:

Most years you can expect to find Wigeon, Teal, Pintail, Goldeneye, Goosander, Divers, Grebes, Bittern, Fieldfare, Redwing, Siskin, Redpoll, Brambling, Waxwing: Jack Snipe are frequent, but easy to overlook!

All year

Common waterfowl, including Mallard, Gadwall, Shoveler, Pochard, Greylag, Canada Goose and Egyptian Goose. Snipe, Oystercatcher, Water Rail, Grey Heron, Little Egret, Kingfisher, Bullfinch, Treecreeper, Buzzard, Kestrel, Red Kite, Sparrowhawk, all five common Crows, Pheasant, Red-legged Partridge, Cetti's Warbler, Tawny Owl, Barn Owl, Little Owl.

Rare or unusual species

The following have all occurred in the Upper Yare Valley on at least one occasion:
American Wigeon, Smew, Scaup, Great Egret, Ring-billed Gull, Snow Bunting, Yellow-browed Warbler.

Yare Valley: Norwich reaches – Eaton to Whitlingham Lane

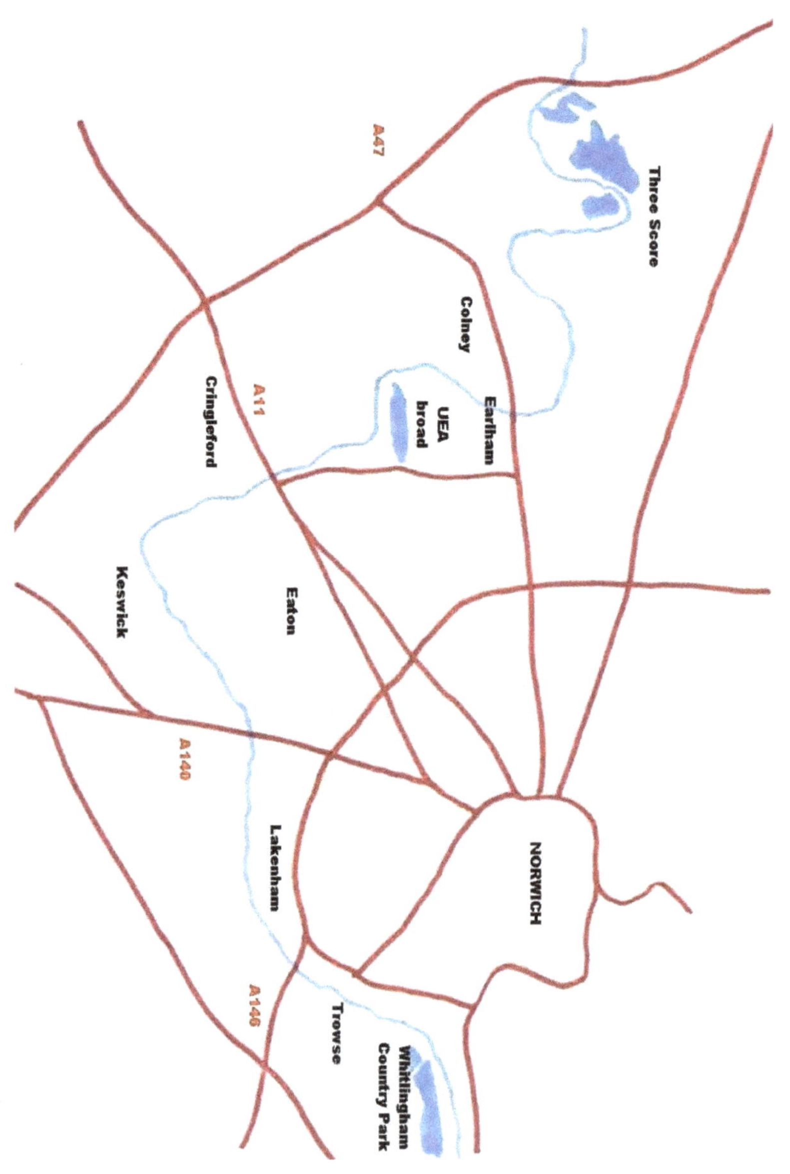

Yare Valley: Norwich reaches – Eaton to Whitlingham Lane

THIS section of the valley lies to the south of the city, running through the villages and suburbs of Cringleford, Keswick and Lakenham and includes several more watermills. There are locations from which the river can be investigated, but much of the area has limited access and remains underwatched.

Cringleford

Some of the meadows and riverbanks in this picturesque village are designated conservation areas or are privately owned. Those reaches that *can* be visited, however, are good for Grey Wagtails, Kingfishers and Reed, Sedge and Cetti's Warblers.

Access is from the car park in Eaton Road, Cringleford: a public footpath passes underneath the A11 to the river, continuing all the way north through Bluebell Marsh to the UEA Broad.

Marston Lane

Along this stretch, the Yare meanders through water meadows, grazing marsh and between occasional belts of woodland. The river holds a good stock of Chub, Dace and Roach, the fry of which provide food for Kingfishers and the occasional Little Egret. A rich variety of fen and marsh plants can be found, and several species of dragonfly and damselfly patrol the river banks.

Access is from the A140: heading south from Norwich, turn right into Marston Lane and park by Danby Wood (Good for woodland species) Approach the river through the kissing gate: the area can be quite boggy at times, so boots are essential.

Other species you might encounter include Snipe, Cetti's Warbler, Cuckoo and Green and Great Spotted Woodpeckers.

Postcode: NR4 6LJ

This Great Egret at Bowthorpe Marsh was present for several years

The 'Pintard' – a Pintail / Mallard hybrid – at Thorpe Green

East Norfolk is an important stronghold for Barn Owls

Siskins are a regular winter visitor to the Yare Valley

Lakenham

From Marston Lane the Yare passes under the A140 Ipswich Road, running parallel with the tiny River Tas before the two meet at Trowse.

There are several points of access, but don't leave valuables in your car – this is a car crime hotspot. When the Tesco Superstore was built, a wildlife conservation area with hide was constructed: sadly the hide was quickly vandalised and burnt down. However, at the time of writing, there is still access to the water meadows and small pond via the Tesco car park.

The most productive part of this area is reached from Stoke Road, straight over the mini-roundabout by the Cock Public House (Now closed) The Yare can be viewed from the road bridge by the pub and Grey Wagtails and warblers are frequently seen or heard. Before the railway bridge there is a small green on the left with some parking. Carry on over the bridge and the footpath starts on the left of the road. This section holds a respectable population of breeding birds, but is particularly good for dragonflies and damselflies. In the south eastern corner of the rough field – although sadly invisible! – is the Arminghall Woodhenge, the most important monument of its kind in eastern England. Barn Owls are not infrequently seen hunting over the meadows at dawn or dusk.

Further access is via Cooper Lane, a narrow road leading from the right-hand bend in Sandy Lane, Lakenham. If travelling by car, the road by the shops in Sandy Lane is the nearest place to park. At the very end of Cooper Lane is a somewhat overgrown meadow with a path leading to the river. Species here include Reed, Sedge and Cetti's Warblers, Reed Bunting and, occasionally, Kingfisher. Barn Owls are seen on the opposite side of the river.

Postcode: NR1 2LY

Trowse

Here the River Yare completes the final stage of its journey to a confluence with the River Wensum. Flowing under the A146 through water meadows and a converted watermill complex at Bracondale, the riverbanks next become accessible from Whitlingham Lane, just past the dry ski slope. One of the region's most astonishing vagrants – a Black and White Warbler – spent a week hiding in the trees here in November, 1996. Nearctic passerines are, for obvious reasons, rarely encountered in East Anglia and are often suspected of being ship-assisted. However, with an earlier record not far away at How Hill, Ludham, most observers (including me!) were happy enough to add it to their patch lists. More regular are the usual waterfowl and woodland species.

Just to the west of Whitlingham Country Park, the Yare joins with the much larger Wensum: by some quirk of the medieval Norfolk mind, the resulting river is called the Yare for the remainder of its journey to the North Sea.

Whitlingham Country Park

This two lake complex includes the Norwich Outdoor Activities Centre, and canoeing and sailing frequently take place on the Great Broad. There is an Information Centre and restaurant in a converted flint barn by one of the numerous pay and display car parks, which make the Park a popular destination for dog walkers, picnickers and families. Nevertheless, the five kilometre circular walk around the Great Broad takes in some good stands of woodland, scrub and reed fringing and the broad itself has produced some excellent birds over the years. In fact, over two hundred species have been recorded, including such waterfowl as Velvet Scoter, Common Scoter, Green-winged Teal, Ferruginous Duck, Ring-necked Duck and all three sawbills, as well as all five British Grebes. In addition to the illustrious 'Yank' noted earlier, passerine species have included Golden Oriole, Marsh Warbler and Yellow-browed Warbler: more usual woodland birds are Siskin and Linnet. At least one of each of the UK raptor species has been seen over the Broad and, in May 2014, from my stationary car I watched what I am still convinced was a Booted Eagle soaring low over the nearby A47.

Postcode: NR14 8TR

Thorpe Marsh

On the other side of the River Yare, to the east of Whitlingham Country Park, is a similar area of open water, dykes and water meadows. This can be reached from the A1242, old Yarmouth Road. Since the creation of Norfolk's version of Spaghetti Junction at Postwick, directions are by no means straight forward! Heading east along the A47 south of Norwich, follow the signs to the Broadland Business Park, turning left off the southern by-pass and first left onto the A1042 at the roundabout. Follow this road over a couple more roundabouts and under a low railway bridge. At the mini-roundabout, go left on the A1242 until you see a set of traffic lights. Park on the road before these, then continue on foot, turning left past the lights down *another* Whitlingham Lane. At the end is a pedestrian railway bridge: Thorpe Marsh Reserve is the other side of this! There is a circular walk of around two kilometres that allows views of the Broad across wide reed fringes: wildfowl can be a little distant! Species you might encounter here are pretty much identical to those at Whitlingham Country Park, with the possible addition of Nightingale as a recent breeding species.

Postcode: NR7 0QA

Thorpe Green

Were you to carry on along the A1242 for a kilometre or so, you would come to an attractive grassy area on the banks of a narrow stretch of water. This channel loops around an island to the north of the Yare and is a popular place for families to feed waterfowl and gulls. From time to time Mediterranean Gulls have taken up residence here and, if present, may be enjoyed at close range. Another interesting individual has been a drake Mallard / Pintail hybrid: a surprisingly handsome and photogenic fellow!

Parking is in a long layby just before the green, where, at the time of writing, there is an excellent little cafe!

Birds of the Norwich reaches

Spring:

Migrating birds following the River Yare frequently stop off in this region to feed or re-orientate: the larger bodies of water are the best places to look for them. Regular visitors are Osprey, Black and Arctic Tern, and Whimbrel.

Summer:

Breeding birds may include Garganey, Common Tern, Little Ringed Plover Blackcap, Whitethroat, Lesser Whitethroat, Willow Warbler, Chiff-chaff, Reed Warbler, Sedge Warbler, Grasshopper Warbler and, some years, Nightingale.

Autumn

Autumn passage can often be the more productive in this part of the Yare Valley and failed breeding birds generally stay a little longer. Unusual waders and warblers and Shrikes are all worth looking out for.

Winter:

Diligent searching of large waters such as Whitlingham Great Broad often pays dividends in the winter: regular wildfowl such as Wigeon, Teal, Mallard, Gadwall and Shoveler are frequently joined by Pintail, Goldeneye, Smew and Goosander, while Divers and the rarer Grebes are annual. Jack Snipe, Bittern, Fieldfare, Redwing, Siskin, Redpoll, Brambling, Waxwing all occur.

All year

Common waterfowl, including Mallard, Gadwall, Shoveler, Pochard, Greylag, Canada Goose and Egyptian Goose are widespread, while waders include Snipe, Oystercatcher and Redshank. Grey Heron and Little Egret may be encountered almost anywhere, while Kingfisher, Grey Wagtail, Treecreeper and Bullfinch (while present) are generally less predictable. Suitable habitat can produce Buzzard, Kestrel, Red Kite, Sparrowhawk, all five common Crows, Pheasant, Red-legged Partridge, Cetti's Warbler, Tawny Owl, Barn Owl and Little Owl. Water Rail are abundant, but, like Cetti's Warblers, are more often heard than seen!

Common Cranes are increasingly frequent visitors from their stronghold in the east of the county, and groups of up to a dozen have been seen flying over Lakenham.

Rare or unusual species

The following have all occurred in the Norwich reaches of the Yare Valley on at least one occasion:

Scaup, Velvet Scoter, Red-crested Pochard, Ring-necked Duck, Great Egret, Spoonbill, Ring-billed Gull, Snow Bunting, Yellow-browed Warbler,
Black and White Warbler.

The Mid Yare Valley:
Postwick to Cantley

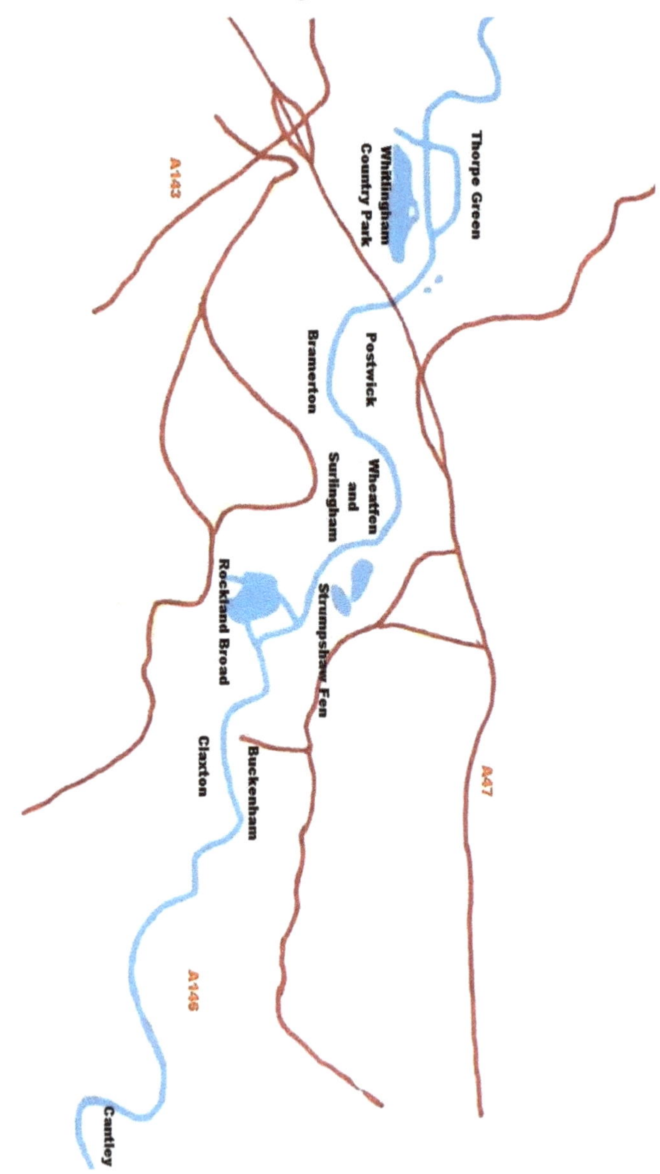

The Mid Yare Valley: Postwick to Cantley

THE mid-Yare region is arguably the most productive stretch of the valley. There are several attractive reserves and plenty of areas of reedbed and woodland on both sides of the river. Marsh Harriers, Hobbies, Kingfishers and Bitterns are regular and this is one of the best places in the UK to see Swallowtail butterflies.

For simplicity, the location details below follow the river downstream, hopping from bank to bank! The stretch of the Yare from Postwick to Brundall provides opportunities to connect with a good range of species: at the moment easy access both north and south of the river is possible at a number of locations, but this may change with the completion of the housing development at Postwick.

Bramerton

This attractive stretch on the southern bank of the river holds a good variety of waterfowl, woodland birds and fly-over raptors. From the A47 take the A146 Loddon Road: take the first left (Kirby Road) In Kirby Bredon, take the left turn along Mill Hill. Pass the pub (or not, as you wish!) and park on the left by the riverside green. Popular with anglers, holiday makers and picnickers, this area is best visited out of season or early in the day.

Postcode: NR14 7ED

Postwick

Heading east on the A47 southern bypass, follow the signs to Postwick through the somewhat convoluted string of roundabouts. Passing the Park and Ride on your right, turn into Oaks Lane at yet another roundabout.

Sedge Warblers are one of the earliest migrants to arrive

Common Snipe are present in the Yare Valley throughout the year

Cetti's Warblers are resident throughout the Yare Valley

Bitterns are frequent visitors but only occasional breeders

There is a small layby on the right by the entrance to as tarmac cycle path: this allows views of a small flooded drainage pool that often hold gulls and waders, including unusual species at times.

At the end of Oaks Lane, turn left past Postwick Village Hall along Ferry Lane. After half a kilometre there is a right turn that leads to a small car park. There is a footpath here that follows the river westwards: Kingfisher, waterfowl (including occasional Mandarins) Marsh Harrier, Cuckoo and most of the expected warbler species are regular.

Postcode: NR13 5NP

Surlingham Church Marsh

The circular walk around the marsh, pools and reedbeds of this compact RSPB reserve can be quite good for all the regular species: Kingfisher, Water Rail, and Marsh Harrier. Barn, Tawny and Little Owls have been recorded, and Hobby is regular in the summer. Winter visitors might be lucky enough to encounter Hen Harrier and Bittern, but neither are guaranteed! From Surlingham village, drive along Walnut Hill for a kilometre and then turn right into Church Lane. From the church there is a footpath leading down to the reserve.

Postcode: NR14 7DF

Wheatfen Broad: the Ted Ellis Trust

More than any other individual, Ted Ellis was the Norfolk naturalist who not only discovered the importance of the Broads as a unique wildlife habitat, but also correctly identified their origins as medieval peat diggings. As with Surlingham, the reserve has a circular path (which can be muddy in the winter) around woodland, marsh and open water. It holds the same species as Church Marsh, but can be better for Bearded Tit, especially in the winter. As is the case with all the mid-Yare reedbeds, Swallowtails can be encountered from May onwards, and it is not so much the birdlife that is of interest to visitors but rather the many species of unusual invertebrates and plants that may be found here.

From Surlingham village, drive east and turn right at the crossroads. Continue along The Covey for a kilometre until you reach the car park

Postcode: NR14 7AL

The Yare Valley is a nationally important site for Swallowtails

Once a rare bird, Marsh Harriers are regular at all the Yare reserves

The pig-like squealing of Water Rails is heard throughout the valley

A Swallowtail caterpillar feeding on Milk Parsley

This shallow, tidal broad can be visited by driving south from Surlingham along Mill Road to the village of Rockland St Mary. Turn left to the eastern end of the village: opposite the New Inn PH is a small marina with a dyke leading to the broad. From here there is a footpath to the right of the dyke that leads around the south and east of Rockland Broad to a birdwatching hide maintained by the RSPB. This overlooks the broad and has provided views of some astonishing birds in the past, including Whiskered and White-winged Black Terns. Osprey is regular in the Autumn, while from the Wherryman's Way that leads east to Claxton Hen Harrier, Barn Owl and Short-eared Owl are seen hunting over the marshes in the winter. Rockland Broad is shot over by wildfowlers in the winter, so it's best to avoid Fridays and Saturdays.

Postcode: NR14 7HP

Brundall Gardens and Brundall

The road from the A47 to Postwick passes to the north of the Yare through farmland and copse to the village of Brundall. Just before the village is the railway halt at Brundall Gardens: here a footpath crosses the railway by a footbridge, continues west along the railway, before heading south to the river. Here and there are patches of damp woodland that may be explored, although the majority are private. Both Pied and Spotted Flycatcher have been seen here, as well as Nightingale: if you're in the area in the spring, it's definitely worth a look.

Brundall itself is a centre for the Broads holiday trade and has a marina, supermarkets, pubs, restaurants and an excellent Chinese takeaway!

It also has its own Local Nature Reserve: Church Fen. Until recently this was an inaccessible jungle, but it has been opened up and cleared and has become a pleasant – and occasionally productive – place to visit. The main attraction is the rich variety of plant life, but the scrub and reedbeds hold Cetti's, Reed and Sedge Warbler, while Tawny Owls are frequently heard at dusk. For two years in the nineties my wife Linda and I owned a house in Brundall that overlooked the river valley: the list of birds we saw from the small back garden was incredible and included Goshawk, Osprey, Hen &

Marsh Harrier and Waxwing. On two occasions we heard the characteristic 'whiplash' call of a Spotted Crake, so the potential of the boatyards and Church Fen shouldn't be underestimated.

Postcode: NR13 5RG

Strumpshaw Fen RSPB Reserve

Considered by many to be the jewel in the crown of the Yare Valley, this compact reserve has an enviable list of species seen. Being a fair way inland from the North Sea, bird density is not high, so regular visits are necessary to get the most from this location. This may well be the best place in the UK for Marsh Harriers: they often come within a few metres of the hides! Breeding species include Bittern, Marsh Harrier, Cuckoo, Bearded Tit, Grasshopper Warbler, Water Rail, Tawny, Barn and Little Owl and Kingfisher, while the reserve is probably the easiest location in Norfolk to see Willow Emerald Damselfly, Norfolk Hawker and Scarce Chaser. An introduction scheme has resulted in a good population of Raft Spiders, but you may have to book a walk with a warden to see one! Swallowtails and White Admiral butterflies are, however, usually easy to find in the early summer. Hobbies, Buzzards and Peregrines are frequently encountered, while exotic Reeve's Pheasants are not unusual here.

Stoat and Chinese Water Deer are common and Otters are frequently encountered, particularly in the winter. Scarce or unusual birds in recent years have included Wryneck, Caspian Tern, Great Northern Diver, Common Crane, Great Egret, Spoonbill, Glossy Ibis, Savi's Warbler, Great Grey and Red-backed Shrike, Osprey, Montagu's and Hen Harrier, while Penduline Tits have summered several years in a row. A good variety of waders are seen on passage when water levels are suitably low and have included Little Stint, Wood, Green and Common Sandpiper and Whimbrel. Sadly, Willow Tit and Lesser Spotted Woodpecker have disappeared, while Nuthatch is now an irregular breeder.

From Brundall, take the Strumpshaw Road east from the village, passing under a low railway bridge. Take the turning on the right (Stone Road) towards the recycling centre, then immediately right along Low Road to the reserve.

Penduline Tilts have visited Strumpshaw Fen on several occasions

Common Cranes may soon breed in the Yare Valley

Willow Emerald damselflies are now widespread in the Yare Valley

White Admirals are a feature of the Woodland Walk at Strumpshaw

Little Owls are regular breeders throughout the mid-Yare Valley

Up to four Great Grey Shrikes visited Strumpshaw in October 2015

A pair of Peregrine Falcons on a chimney at Cantley Sugar Factory

Whinchats are fairly regular on passage at Buckenham Marsh

There is ample car parking on both sides of the road: access to Strumpshaw Fen is across a pedestrian railway crossing through a white-painted wooden gate. It's really important to look both ways – trains here are fast and frequent!

The reserve centre has clean, modern toilets, a tea and coffee machine and overlooks an expanse of shallow water. Almost every species you might expect at Strumpshaw Fen can be seen here: it is generally the best place to look for Otters and Kingfishers. A small 'dipping pool' behind the bird feeders is often good for Small Red-eyed Damselfly.

Swallowtails frequently feed on the wild flower garden by the reserve centre in late May and June, while most years Bee Orchids can be seen among the grass by the path.

During the winter months, when the easterly winds blow across the muddy paths and reed beds, it is possible to spend the whole day here and meet just a few hardy locals: however, from Easter onwards it's a different story! The RSPB seems to have identified the reserve as ideal for development as a family and education-oriented complex. There are plans for new hides, a shop and café (along the lines of Minsmere and Titchwell) and increased public outreach. It is to be hoped that these ambitions don't destroy the character of this charming place, nor spoil its attraction for wildlife.

Postcode: NR13 4HS

Buckenham Marsh RSPB reserve

In December this can be a cold, desolate place! Nevertheless, it's worth a visit for the regular flock of Taiga Bean Geese and the huge numbers of Pink-footed and White-fronted Geese, Wigeon, Fieldfares, Redwings and Golden Plover that over-winter here. The huge corvid roost in December and January can be an impressive sight! All year round the marshes are patrolled by,Buzzards, Marsh Harriers and Peregrines (which breed on nearby Cantley Beet Factory) while Hobbies, Ruff and Avocet are annual in the spring and summer. Passerines include Linnet, Stonechat, Whinchat, Cetti's Warber and Cuckoo. Yellow Wagtails and Garganey, too, are seen most years, while rarities have included American Wigeon, White-tailed Eagle, Honey Buzzard, Pacific Golden Plover, Pectoral Sandpiper, Caspian

Strumpshaw Fen RSPB reserve

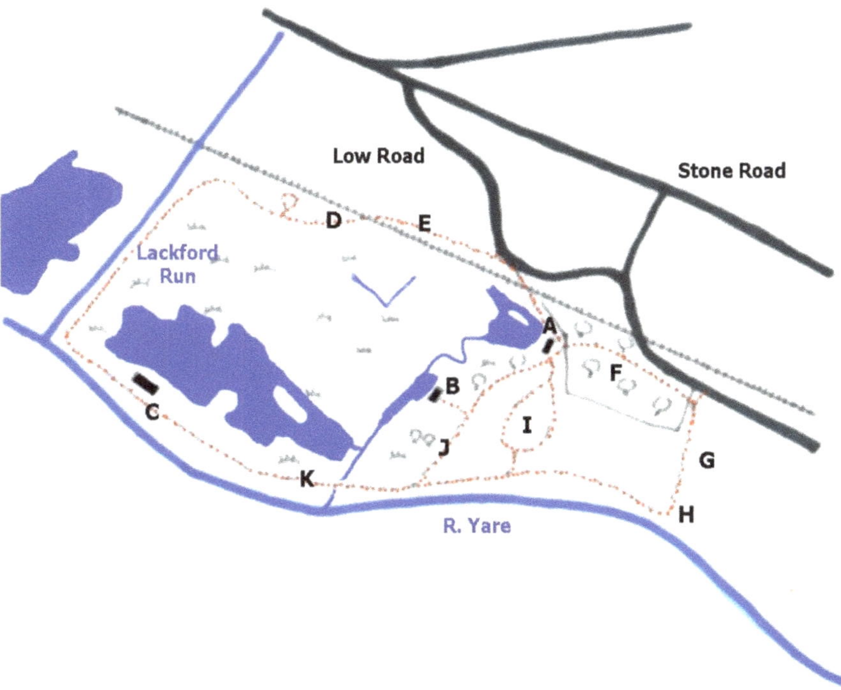

A Reception and toilets

B Fen Hide – Bittern, Marsh Harrier, Kingfisher

C Tower Hide – Terns, waders, wildfowl, Bittern

D Best area for Willow Emeralds

E Cottage Garden – Swallowtails and Brown Argus

F Woodland Walk – White Admirals and Grass Snakes

G Gravel Path – Stonechat, Hobby, Barn Owl

H Drainage Pump

I Meadow Trail – Dragonflies, Damselflies, Orchids

J Sandy Path – Grasshopper Warbler, Bearded Tit

K Sluice and riverside – Cetti's and other warblers

Tern, Red-footed Falcon, Montagu's Harrier, White Stork, Common Crane, Spoonbill and Great Egret.

Buckenham Marshes can be reached from Strumpshaw by driving east from the car park, turning right at the 'T' junction and waiting for the level crossing to be opened for you! Drive on to the Station, following the road down to the river where there is a hide and small anglers' car park. A short walk east along the river bank to a derelict drainage mill gives views across a large, shallow pool that can be excellent for wildfowl and waders. Alternatively, drive back to Stone Road and turn right past the recycling centre (Strumpshaw Hill on the left is good for warblers, owls and, occasionally, Grey Partridge). Turn right down the hill and right again before the Red Barn: there is an RSPB car park by the railway station.

Postcode: NR13 4HW

Claxton Marshes

This area of rough grazing and reed-filled dykes has been celebrated in the books and newspaper articles of a local author. His evocative writings captured the wild beauty of the region and awoke many to its exceptional birding potential.

The marshes can be reached by walking east from Rockland along the Wherryman's Way or by driving to Claxton and turning left just past a beautiful carving of a Barn Owl. There is very limited parking, so don't obstruct tracks or farm gates. The track continues along the river bank all the way back to Rockland, and the car park by Rockland Boat Dyke is another point of access.

Star birds are the winter-visiting Short-eared Owls: in some years there can be a double figure population hunting among the tussock sedge. Calm, frosty mornings seem to be best: view from the raised path leading down to the river (try to find some cover if possible – the Owls will come very close if they don't see you!).

Other regular species include Buzzard, Whooper and Bewick Swan, Marsh and Hen Harrier, Barn Owl and Golden Plover, while migrating waders such as Whimbrel pass through on passage. Red-footed Falcon, Rough-legged Buzzard and Montagu's Harrier have all been recorded in recent years.

Stonechats are widespread from the mid-Yare Valley to the sea

Avocets – once a very rare visitor – can now be seen all year

Four Garganey at Strumpshaw Fen – a regular migrant and breeder

A long-staying Wryneck on the riverbank at Strumpshaw in 2013

Nuthatch at Strumpshaw Fen (Brian Shreeve)

Treecreeper at Strumpshaw Fen (Brian Shreeve)

Reed Warbler at Strumpshaw Fen (Brian Shreeve)

Water Pipit at Strumpshaw Fen (Brian Shreeve)

Recently a Black Redstart spent a day or two on the roofs of the Beauchamp Arms: this species is probably under-recorded in the Yare Valley.

Postcode: NR14 7AS

Cantley Marshes

Basically a continuation of Buckenham Marsh, this expanse of grazing meadow, dykes and shallow pools attracts large numbers of wintering wildfowl, including the Taiga Bean Geese. These can often be observed far closer than at Buckenham from the path running south from Burnt House Road: note there is strictly no parking along this narrow residential street. There is some parking by Cantley Station and, a little further along Station Road, opposite the bowling club. From this car park you can walk left, then left again down a concrete track that leads to the river bank. The (often muddy) path runs all the way back to Buckenham, being joined after a mile or so by the track from Burnt House Road. The list of species that has been seen here is a long one, but be aware that some days can be totally unproductive. However, there are always plenty of dragonflies in the summer, including Norfolk and Brown Hawkers, as well as the ubiquitous Chinese Water Deer.

Some years back, the Cantley dykes were the points of release of large numbers of Raft Spiderlings: these have apparently done well, resulting in a healthy population of the UK's largest spider. However, I've yet to find one from the limited access available to the visitor!

As well as the regular wintering geese and duck flocks, other species recorded include White-tailed Eagle, Glossy Ibis, Great Egret, Spoonbill and Iceland Gull.

Cantley Sugar Beet Factory

The settling pools and extensive reedbeds of the British Sugar Corporation factory at Cantley have turned up almost as many rare and unusual birds as some of the better-known Norfolk reserves, while waders such as Wood and Green Sandpipers are guaranteed during spring and autumn passage.

However, the entire site is subject to strict security and entry is granted to only a limited number of visitors at any one time. To obtain a day permit, birders must apply at the Security Office opposite Cantley Station (and remember to hand back the permit and check out on leaving!)

From the security office a well-marked 'safe route' leads to the river and eastwards to the pools. It is important to keep to the paths and follow onsite instructions at all times. While walking through the factory alongside the River Yare, a glance upward will often give views of one of the Peregrines that nest and hunt here, while it is not unusual to glimpse a Kingfisher whirring low over the water.

The most easterly pool has rows of small islands and shallow bays with sandy fringes that attract waders and wildfowl, while the scrub and reedy margins hold warblers and, on occasion, Bearded Tits. There are extensive reedbeds and Bittern certainly over-winter and perhaps occasionally breed: Marsh Harriers are resident, while Hen Harriers are increasingly scarce winter visitors. The whole of the site is excellent for both dragonflies and damselflies and the many Buddleia bushes attract a good variety of butterflies.

Rare or unusual species recorded include Marsh, Baird's, Pectoral and Curlew Sandpiper, White-winged Black, Caspian and Black Tern, Spoonbill, Great Egret, White Stork and Osprey.

Postcode: NR13 3ST

Birds of the Mid Yare Valley

Spring:

In the spring, migrating birds often drop into this region of the Yare Valley: unusual records have included Savi's Warbler, Red-backed Shrike, Penduline Tit, Caspian Tern, White-tailed Eagle and Honey Buzzard. More regular are Osprey, Hobby, Black and Arctic Tern, Whimbrel and Bar-tailed and Black Godwits.

Summer:

Breeding birds include Garganey, Bittern, Common Tern, Little Ringed Plover, Blackcap, Whitethroat, Lesser Whitethroat, Willow Warbler, Chiffchaff, Reed Warbler, Sedge Warbler, Grasshopper Warbler.

Autumn

As with Spring passage, migrating species often break their journies in the Mid Yare Valley: these have included Great Grey Shrike, Pectoral, Green and Wood Sandpiper and Black Redstart

Winter:

At this time of year the grazing marshes hold enormous flocks of Wigeon and Teal that are not infrequently joined by Pintail and Goldeneye, while several times in the past the goose flocks have attracted Lesser White-fronted Goose. Jack Snipe, Bittern, Fieldfare, Redwing, Siskin, Redpoll, Brambling, Waxwing can be found most years. Large pre-dispersal flocks of Bearded Tits are virtually annual at Strumpshaw Fen

All year

Common waterfowl, including Mallard, Gadwall, Shoveler, Pochard, Greylag, Canada Goose and Egyptian Goose are widespread, while waders include Snipe, Oystercatcher and Redshank. Marsh Harrier, Grey Heron and Little Egret can all often be seen at very close range. Grey Partridge is a scarce bird in east Norfolk, but have been seen at Cantley.

The Lower Yare Valley:
Reedham to Breydon Water

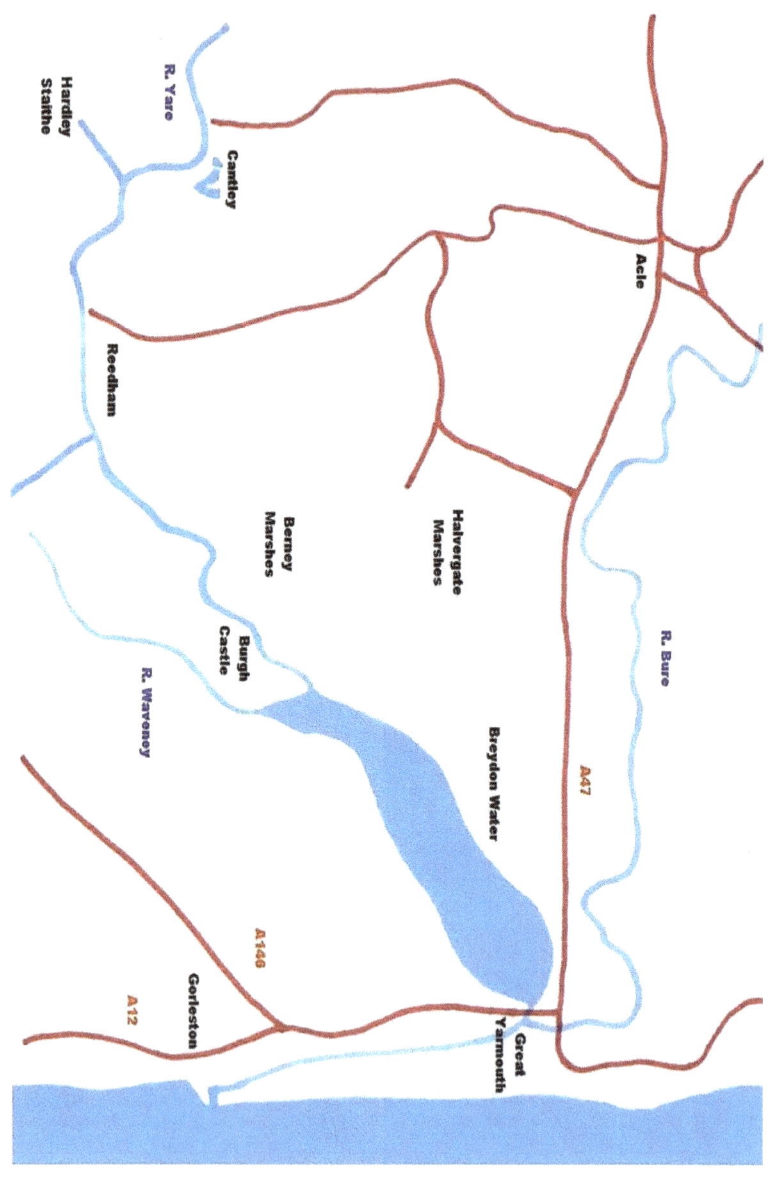

The Lower Yare Valley: Reedham to Breydon Water

OPPOSITE Cantley Beet Factory – but an hour's drive away by car! – is an area of marsh, reedbed, dykes and a small pool that can be very productive, particularly in the winter. Short-eared Owls are frequent (as are Barn and Little Owls all year round) while Rough-legged Buzzards have become a regular feature in recent years. The small pool is private, but can be investigated from the raised river banks by walking westwards from the end of the left bank of Hardley Staithe Dyke. It has hosted sea duck such as Scaup and Goldeneye and, on one recent occasion, a drake Ring-necked Duck.

To visit, drive south east on the A146 from Norwich, turning left to Chedgrave after about fifteen kilometres. Follow Hardley Road and Lower Hardley Road all the way to the staithe and River Yare. There is ample parking and sign-posted footpaths.

Reedham

Reached from Acle by driving south along the Reedham Road, this riverside village has a curious little car ferry that is pulled backwards and forwards across the river by a motorised chain drive. A return ticket costs £7 at the time of writing, but, if you are visiting south Norfolk saves a car journey of around fifty kilometres. The nearby Ferry Boat Inn offers good food in pleasant surroundings. Turning left into the village itself, the raised viewing from the road bridge over the railway provides views over the marshes on the opposite side of the Yare. Although distant, Rough-legged Buzzards, Hen Harriers and Short-eared Owls are seen from here most winters, while Barn Owls and Marsh Harriers hunt over the marshes all year.

The village plays host to a colony of Great Green Bush Crickets: these

Close call for a Short-eared Owl at Halvergate

Drake Ring-necked Duck at Hardley Staithe (Brian Tubby)

Flock of Twite near Berney Arms (Brian Tubby)

Close encounter with a Rough-legged Buzzard

impressive beasts can be seen – or more frequently heard – in any suitable scrub around the village.

Postcode: NR13 3EZ

Berney and Halvergate Marshes

A vast area of grazing marsh, reedswamp and dykes fills the entire gap to the north of the Yare between Reedham and Great Yarmouth. Much of this is inaccessible to casual visitors: however, the marshes east of Halvergate and Wickhampton can be reached on foot, as can the RSPB Berney Marshes reserve. The latter can also be reached by boat, by train from Norwich or Great Yarmouth or on foot from Reedham. The reserve is named after the isolated Berney Arms Inn: sadly this is currently closed, but there is some hope that it may reopen in the future.

Driving east on the A47 Acle to Yarmouth road, turn right opposite the Stracey Arms Windmill over a somewhat 'humpy' railway bridge. (Strictly speaking, this region is in the floodplain of the River Bure, but from the layby to the right of the bridge, and from others along the road south towards Halvergate, Short-eared Owls, Rough-legged Buzzards and wild Swans are seen most winters.)

The road is straight but, because of subsidence, a bit of a switchback with all kinds of odd cambers: after two kilometres it turns abruptly right. On the left of this right-angled bend is a small concrete track that winds its way to a space for half a dozen cars to park: don't obstruct field gates! Barn Owls are regular over the fields along the track, while recently this has become a great place to see Cattle Egrets: up to three together in 2016.

In the winter, vast flocks of Pink-footed Geese (with occasional White-fronts) drop onto the marsh to feed, while White Storks (generally agreed to be wire-hoppers from Thrigby Zoo!) are seen most days.

From the 'car park' a footpath leads from the right of the cattle pens all the way to the Berney Arms reserve: this is signposted, but beware – the local farmers are not averse to putting a bull or two into the fields you have to cross! The walk is quite long (around twelve kilometres) but can be enlivened by good views of a variety of birds and other wildlife, including Marsh and Hen Harrier and Bittern. Winter thrushes are often abundant and the shallow pools on the grazing marsh have held Glossy Ibis, including a flock of five in 2012. The Pink-footed Goose flock occasionally acts as a carrier for more unusual species such as Ross's and Tundra Bean Geese and is always worth checking thoroughly.

Birds of the Lower Yare Valley:

Spring:

Almost *anything* can turn up on migration: the region is comparatively underwatched, so there's no doubt that many unusual birds pass through unnoticed. Regular species include Whimbrel, Yellow Wagtail, White Wagtail, and, recently, Cattle Egret.

Summer:

Breeding birds on the marshes may include Garganey, Redshank, Oystercatcher, Bearded Tit, Bittern, Reed Warbler, Sedge Warbler, Grasshopper Warbler and Reed Bunting.

Autumn

Autumn passage can be very productive in the lower regions of the Yare Valley and failed breeders generally stay a little longer. Glossy Ibis is becoming regular and many unusual waders are probably overlooked.

Winter:

Given that the marshes can be pretty bleak in the winter, there is little doubt that more birds visit the region than are seen and recorded. Among the large flocks of Pink-footed Geese Tundra Beans, Ross's and Snow Geese have been found in the past and it's not impossible that other vagrant species have been overlooked. Good herds of both Bewick and Whooper Swans and vast assemblies of Mute Swans build up on the grazing marsh and arable fields. Short-eared Owl and Rough-legged Buzzard are annual.

All year

All the regular waders, including Snipe, Oystercatcher, Curlew and Redshank can be expected, as can Heron and Little Egret. White Storks on the run from Thrigby Hall are increasingly regular: who knows if the odd unringed bird might be a genuinely wild individual?

Cattle Egrets at Halvergate: part of a flock of four

Unringed White Stork on the Acle Straight, just outside Great Yarmouth

Pink-footed Geese arrive in huge flocks in the Autumn

Juvenile Cuckoo near Wickhampton

Breydon Water to Gorleston

FIVE kilometres short of the North Sea, the River Yare meets the River Waveney and spreads out into the sheltered tidal estuary known as Breydon Water. This is one of the UK's largest areas of protected wetland being around 5 km long and 1.5 km. It has SSSI (Site of Special Scientific Interest) status, largely because of the globally important wader flocks that feed on the exposed mudflats at low tide.

Breydon Water can be viewed from footpaths along both shores, access to the southern bank being from Burgh Castle and to the northern bank from Reedham. Both sides can be reached from Great Yarmouth (See map) Which side you choose largely depends on the time of day, the tides and the weather conditions. On a clear day, viewing from the northern bank is very difficult because of the glare of reflected sunlight: this is, naturally, less of a problem early or late in the day. However, as the tide fills the estuary, the wader flocks are pushed towards the northern shore which has a fringe of saltmarsh at its eastern end. Ultimately, though, the choice made may depend on the last reported location of a scarce or interesting bird! Photography of waders and waterfowl is almost always difficult because of distance and heat haze, but the marshes on both sides of Breydon can provide excellent opportunities to get up close and personal with species such as Twite, Short-eared Owl, Rough-legged Buzzard and both Rock and Water Pipit.

The River Yare flows under the impressive Breydon road bridge, joining the River Bure before passing under Haven Bridge, through the docks and entering the sea.

Burgh Castle and Church Farm Marshes

As mentioned earlier, the estuary of the Yare was much larger in Roman times and, because of its strategic importance, was defended by two Roman

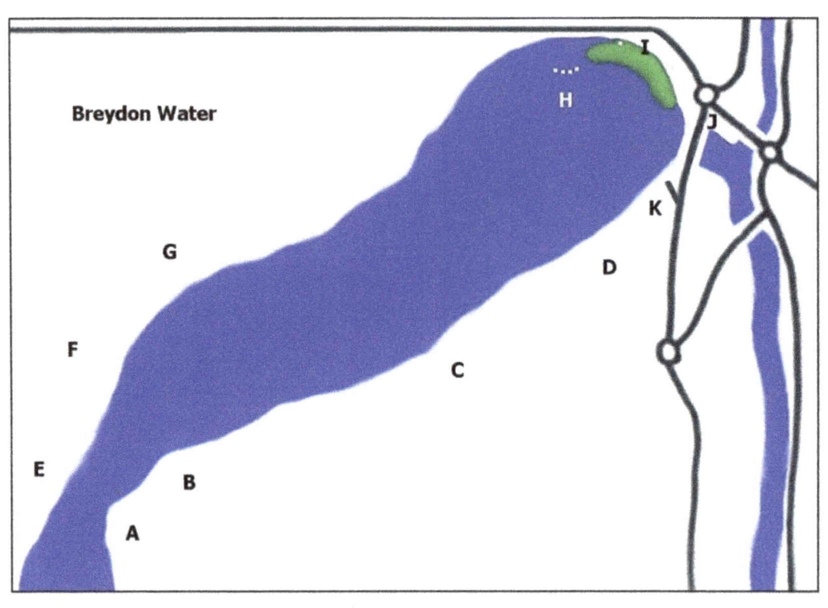

A   **Church Farm Marshes**

B   **Burgh Castle Marshes**

C   **Fisher's Marshes**

D   **Humberstone Marshes**

E   **Reedham Marshes**

F   **Halvergate Marshes**

G   **Acle Marshes**

H   **Tern platforms**

I   **The Lumps and hide**

J   **ASDA - parking for north shore**

K   **Parking for south shore**

forts at Caister and Burgh Castle. Both may be visited, but the substantial flint and brick walls of the latter are the more impressive: they can be seen from across the river at Berney Arms.

The rough grazing and marshland that fringe the south western shore of Breydon Water can be accessed from Burgh Castle: a footpath from

Church Road (where there is parking available) leads west to join the Angles Way, a national pathway that runs along more or less the entire southern shore to Great Yarmouth. As the tide rises, waders and other water birds are pushed into this area and rarities that were discovered at distance at the eastern end of Breydon are frequently relocated here, often at much closer range.

The species seen here are those you would expect over the whole of Breydon and its surrounding marshland: having said which, Burgh Castle has been a magnet in recent years for small flocks of Bee-eaters, while Glossy Ibis and Caspian Tern have both occurred, so this end of the estuary is well worth a visit.

Postcode: NR31 9QG

Humberstone and Fisher's Marshes

The south eastern quarter of Breydon Water is watched much more intensively by a core group of dedicated local patchers, who, as a result, have discovered some incredible birds in recent years. These have included the UK's fourth (or possibly fifth!) Great Knot, Killdeer and both Pacific and American Golden Plovers. Richard's Pipits have been virtually annual on the grazing marsh, but are often elusive in the long coarse grass, while Purple Herons have been seen occasionally in the many dykes that criss-cross the marshes. From here, the edges of 'The Lumps' on the far side of Breydon can be scanned with a telescope, allowing views of birds that often remain frustratingly hidden from observers on the northern shore and hide. Here, too, the rising tide pushes waders in quite close and, with the sun behind you all day, this is generally the better option for photography.

Starting from Yarmouth, the best way to access this area is by driving south on the A12 over the Breydon Bridge. Go right round the roundabout back the way you came, turning left just before the bridge : although there

Godwits and Knot at Breydon Water

Golden Plover at Breydon Water

Grey Seal on Breydon Water

Ring-tailed Hen Harrier at Humperstone Marsh, Breydon

is a sign saying 'Access Only', a right turn after a couple of hundred metres leads to two car parks. (It's worth being conscientious about not leaving anything of value in your car at this location!)

Postcode: NR31 0AY

The North Shore and 'The Lumps'

In the past this was the quickest and most convenient point of access to Breydon, since there was plenty of free parking at the ASDA superstore. At the time of writing birders and walkers are still allowed to park here for a couple of hours and I've been told that longer stays can be sanctioned by the parking attendant – you'd need to clarify this on arrival. Alternatively, it's not a long walk past Vauxhall Station to the riverside from the numerous car parks at the western end of Great Yarmouth.

From the ASDA car park, there is a riverside path leading under the Breydon Bridge: it's worth keeping an eye open for Otters here. To the north of the path is an area of scrubby bushes and grass that is worth a glance as you pass: Red-backed Shrike, Quail, Ring Ouzel, as well as the usual warblers and buntings, have all been seen here.

Continuing westwards you reach a bird watching hide (on stilts!) that overlooks an area of salt marsh, tidal creeks and small islands: this is The Lumps. Despite the distances at which the waders habitually feed and the sun being directly in front for much of the day, an astonishing number of rare or unusual birds have been identified from this viewpoint. These have included Broad-billed and Pectoral Sandpiper, Lesser Yellowlegs, Kentish and American Golden Plover, all three Phalaropes and Caspian Tern.

The hide provides an excellent perspective over Breydon, but it is quite small and, a sad sign of the times, subject to vandalism and 'misuse' (!)

Rarities aside, the north eastern corner of Breydon can hold vast numbers of waders and waterfowl in the winter: flocks of Knot, Golden Plover, Avocets and Godwits whirr over the saltings to escape Peregrines and Merlins, while the bays and channels hold significant winter populations of Wigeon, Teal, Pintail and Shelduck. Sea duck such as Goosander, Merganser, Scoter and Scaup are regular, as are Short-eared Owls and Kingfishers.

Carrying on westwards, the path passes four wooden platforms, upon which Common Terns nest. The number of pairs using these is decreasing at the time of writing, largely because of competition with Black-headed Gulls. Nevertheless, the mudflats often hold good numbers of Common, Sandwich and even Little Terns as the tide falls, and Black Terns are reported on passage most years.

The Wherryman's Way footpath continues all the way to the Berney Arms and Reedham, and provides access to some excellent wildlife habitat. To the north of the path lies Signalbox Dyke, which often holds interesting water birds: over the years I have videoed four different species of Grebe here: Great Crested, Little, Red-necked and Slavonian. The reed fringes are good for Reed and Sedge Warbler, Bearded Tit and Reed Bunting, while the foreshore holds Rock Pipit and Twite in the winter.

The main reason birders venture this far in the winter, though, is for the opportunity to watch Rough-legged Buzzards and Short-eared Owls patrolling the grazing marsh. In some years both can be quite easy to connect with, while at other times they fail to arrive at the end of the autumn. Vast flocks of Pink-footed Geese are much more predictable and their yelping calls are a familiar sound-track to a winter walk around Breydon.

Postcode: NR30 1SF

Bure Park

Lying as it does on the east bank of the River Bure, this area of mown grass, scrub and shallow pools isn't strictly a Yare Valley site! However, its proximity to Great Yarmouth means it deserves a mention.

Despite being popular with families and dog walkers, the reed-fringed pool to the south of the car park has held Glossy Ibis, Garganey and Smew and, in 1992, hosted Norfolk's second Ring-billed Gull. In the autumn it's often worth checking the bushes and trees for migrants: Redstart, Yellow-browed Warbler, Whinchat and Pied Flycatcher have all been recorded here.

The park commands a decent view over the River Bure and the marshes beyond and, particularly in the winter, can be worth a look: Pink-footed Geese, Short-eared Owls and waders have all been seen.

Reached by driving north along the A149 Caister Road for about a kilometre, the park is on the left. There is ample free car parking.

Postcode: NR30 4DL

Glossy Ibis at Bure Park

Female ('redhead') Smew at Bure Park

St Nicholas' cemetary

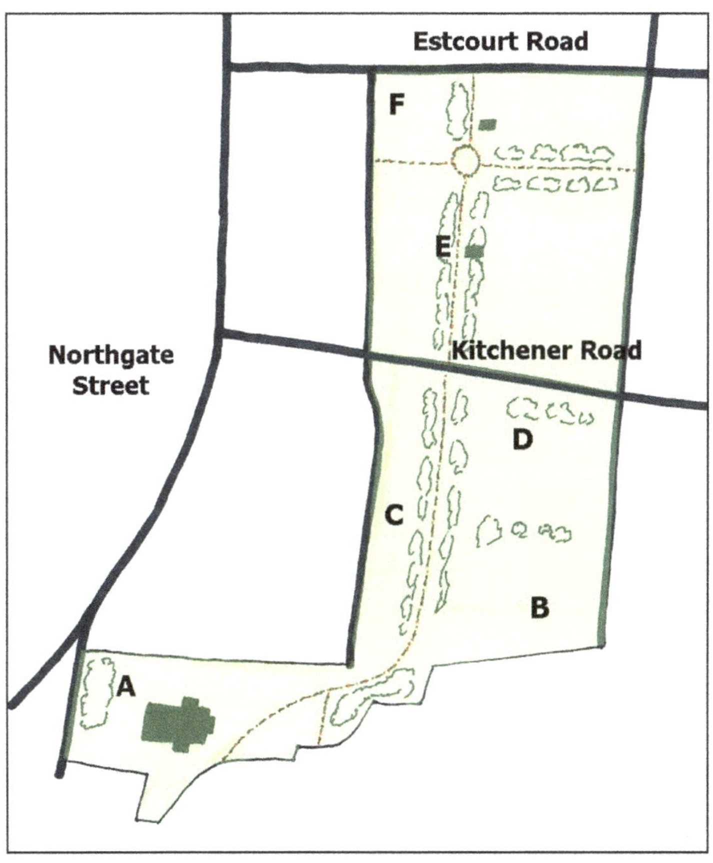

A	Tall trees - often good for warblers and flycatchers
B	Check old gravestones for Redstart and thrushes
C	Rough grass can be good for Ring Ouzel, pipits and chats
D	Conifers attract crests and warblers on passage
E	Sycamores around chapels can hold warblers and flycatchers
F	This corner has produced most of the best rarities!

St Nicholas Churchyard

The impressive Minster Church of St Nicholas is the largest parish church in the UK and dates back to Norman times. Divided into two sections by Kitchener Road, it stands in a large cemetery with plenty of mature trees and bushes: these attract migrants in both spring and autumn and the list of rarities discovered here is a long one.

Searching the two halves methodically can be a long process: birds suddenly pop up in bushes you've been watching for half an hour or flit from branch to branch in the canopy of sycamores high above your head. The most productive way of working the area is to walk slowly along all the main paths, listening for unfamiliar or interesting song or calls. The grassy areas of both sectors have isolated laurel bushes: these are worth spending a few minutes watching from a distance, since they sometimes hold something really special! The rows of sycamore and large yew trees can also be very productive during migration.

It has to be said that, in the heat of a twitchy moment, some birders appear to forget that they are in a cemetery: although many of the internments are very old, the location is sanctified ground and should be treated with respect. Another thing to bear in mind is that some of Great Yarmouth's less salubrious residents occasionally use the cemetery to enjoy the odd can of beer: try to avoid being confrontational!

Given the phenomenal list of rare and unusual species that have turned up in the cemetery, nowadays it is somewhat underwatched compared to past years. Perhaps modern birders are more inclined to sit at home and wait for their pager or phone app. to alert them, or perhaps the surroundings are a bit gothic for some tastes: personally I find the site peaceful and full of potential.

Birds recorded here include Radde's, Yellow-browed, Dusky and Pallas's Warblers, Red-breasted, Pied, Spotted and – perhaps – Collared Flycatchers, Red-flanked Bluetail, Firecrest, Olive-backed Pipit, Hawfinch, Long-eared Owl and Great Grey Shrike!

From Northgate Street, park in Kitchener Road and enter either section of the cemetery via wrought iron gates – the northern side tends to be the most productive, but interesting birds can turn up anywhere!

Postcode: NR30 4HU

North Denes and the Waterways

To the east of St Nicholas Cemetery between the coast road and the North Sea can be found several areas of the town that often produce good birds at all seasons. A curious vintage tourist attraction known as the Venetian Waterways (scheduled for a complete restoration at the time of writing) often attracts interesting seabirds, including Mediterranean and Glaucous Gulls, while the bowling greens and mowed areas can be good for Pied, White, Grey and even Yellow Wagtails. The nearby football pitch and recreation ground can be equally good at times.

Between the Waterways and the North Sea is an extensive area of sand dunes and maram grass that has, in the past, produced some astonishing birds, including a pair of Caspian Plover in May, 1890. These days more likely species might include Shorelark, Snow Bunting, Twite, Stonechat and various species of pipit. Sadly the once thriving Little Tern colony that formerly existed has moved northward to Winterton: even here the pressure from the vast numbers of dog walkers who exercise their pets on the beach is having a negative effect on breeding success.

Seafront

Great Yarmouth seafront can be pretty busy from Easter onwards: nevertheless, there are interesting birds to be found, but an early start is necessary! Common, Sandwich and, less often, Little and Black Terns can all be watched flying past, while Kittiwake and Skuas are worth looking out for in the autumn.

In the winter, however, Marine Parade can be virtually deserted: parking is no problem and disturbance is at a minimum. The seashore between the two piers at the rear of the Sea Life Centre can be absolutely incredible for Mediterranean Gulls – I have counted over one hundred of various ages on several occasions – so it's worth buying a cheap loaf at one of the supermarkets. Glaucous Gulls have been regular winter visitors in recent years and, like the Meds, happily come to bread! In the winter a stroll to the water's edge (or along one of the two piers if either is open) can reward a patient birder with divers, seaduck, grebes, and gannets, as well as Sanderling and other common waders.

Mediterranean Gull on the beach at Great Yarmouth

Turnstone on the promenade behind Great Yarmouth Marina

Glaucous Gull on the seafront rooftops, Great Yarmouth

Snow Buntings on the maram at North Denes

South Denes

South of the Pleasure Beach (a somewhat dated amusement park built in the early years of the twentieth century) and east of the harbour complex lies an area of scrubby dunes and industrial sites. Originally a fishing port packed with drifters and luggers, Great Yarmouth has reinvented itself a number of times: in the nineteen fifties and sixties, with the decline of the herring fishery, the town attempted to become an east coast version of Blackpool. Then, in the seventies, the 'North Sea Oil Boom' brought prosperity to the region, with cutting-edge technology companies and oil rig fabricators taking over much of the harbour area. At the time of writing the southern-most part of South Denes is dominated by the new gas-fired power station and the complex associated with the Outer Harbour. For many years it has seemed that Great Yarmouth cannot decide whether to be a holiday resort or an industrial centre: as a result it possibly fails to achieve either identity. The various buildings – particularly the older, more dilapidated ones – often hold Black Redstarts which may well breed on occasion. Although probably underwatched, the areas of scrub behind the chain-link fencing attract spring migrants such as Redstart, Wheatear, Stonechat and Whinchat and winter visitors including Snow Bunting and Shorelark. More regular are Linnet, Skylark and Meadow Pipit. The roofs of the industrial units hold large flocks of gulls and these are always worth checking: Mediterranean Gulls are frequent, while other white winged species are discovered occasionally.

Harbour Mouth

As the River Yare finally reaches the sea, it divides the two resort towns of Great Yarmouth and Gorleston. The Yarmouth side of the river mouth can be viewed by driving through the harbour along South Denes Road, while from Gorleston follow Riverside Road to Gorleston Pier.

The mouth of the river is not actually that wide and close views can sometimes be had of some interesting species. The scrubby grass by the turning circle on the north side of the river holds Meadow Pipits, Goldfinches and other common species, but it can throw up the occasional surprise: in the early eighties I found an Ortolan Bunting there! Looking across at the Gorleston side can be very productive for gulls: in the winter these have frequently included Glaucous and Mediterranean Gulls, while Kittiwakes can be seen in the summer. Gorleston pier, on the south side of the river is easier to 'work' since there is a concrete pier affording great views out to sea, into the river mouth and south towards Lowestoft. Waders such as Turnstone, Ringed Plover and Redshank often feed on the small, sandy patches under the old wooden jetty on the Yarmouth side, while more unusual species such as Purple Sandpiper and Rock Pipit occasionally turn up in the winter.

Almost any seabird you can think of has been seen on or from Gorleston Pier: the list includes Razorbill, Guillemot, Little Auk, Kittiwake, Glaucous, Iceland and Sabine's Gulls, Shag, Great Northern, Black-throated and Red-throated Divers, Common and Velvet Scoter, Eider, Long-tailed Duck, Manx, Pomarine and Sooty Shearwater and Storm and Leach's Petrels. To be honest, the majority of these records were the result of regular watching by local 'patchers': however, a strong winter easterly is certain to produce at least a few of these species.

Gorleston

It's interesting to note how, in late Victorian times, seaside resorts tended to develop in pairs: usually one of the pair was brash and liberally provided with amusement arcades, 'Kiss-me-Quick' hats and chip stalls, while the other attempted to promote a more refined image, with tea rooms, band-stands and tennis courts. Clacton and Walton, Cromer and Sheringham, Sidmouth and Seaton are existing examples of the phenomenon. Fifty years ago Gorleston was very much the classier neighbour to Great Yarmouth, with hundreds of immaculate Guest Houses and Hotels, a theatre and a dance hall, a yacht pond and a delightful promenade with floral gardens. The decline of the UK seaside holiday trade has, to some extent, taken Gorleston with it, but it still has a certain appeal, especially out of season.

The Promenade and low scrubby 'cliffs' at its southern end have produced some terrific birds, including Desert Wheatear, Booted Warbler, Dusky Warbler, Wryneck: anything is possible during migration periods. More regular at the right time of year are Snow Bunting, Rock and Meadow Pipit and Waxwing, while the seawatch here has produced all the birds listed from the river mouth above, as well as a Black-browed Albatross on one occasion!

Desert Wheatear at Gorleston

Iceland Gull

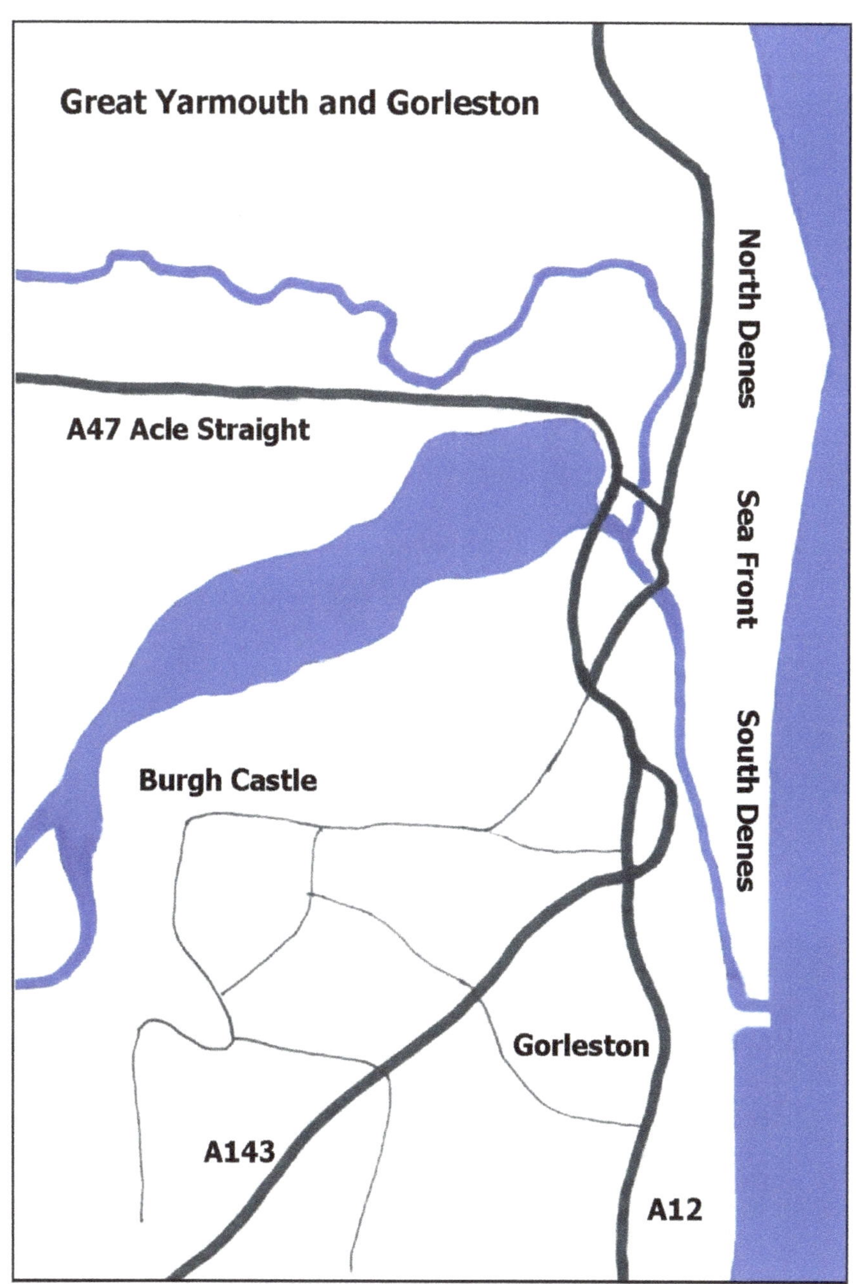

Great Yarmouth and Gorleston
North Denes
Sea Front
South Denes
A47 Acle Straight
Burgh Castle
Gorleston
A143
A12

Checklist of Yare Valley bird species

The following is a list of birds known to have occurred in the Yare Valley: some very old records have been excluded if there is doubt about their reliability.

The movement of birds around the planet is complex and, even now, not fully understood: the chart below is intended as a simplified explanation of the status awarded to each species in the checklist, based on time of year and frequency of its occurrences in the Yare Valley

The blank column is for you to keep your own records, should you wish!

Resident	**A bird that normally spends the whole year in one location without migrating.**
Weather movement	**During prolonged bad weather, resident species may relocate to regions with more favourable conditions**
Migrant	**A bird that passes from one part of the globe to another on a regular route: it may linger for a time to feed before moving on**
Vagrant	**A bird that takes a wrong course during migration and appears some distance from its usual summer or winter destinations: it may well remain until the next migration**
Irruptive species	**A bird that occasionally disperses from areas where it is usually resident: this may be because of a successful breeding season resulting in over-population, or a failure of the chosen food items**

Red-throated Diver	Common in winter	
Black-throated Diver	Scarce in winter	
Great Northern Diver	Scarce in winter	
Little Grebe	Widespread	
Great Crested Grebe	Widespread	
Red-necked Grebe	Scarce in winter and on passage	
Slavonian Grebe	Scarce in winter and on passage	
Black-necked Grebe	Scarce in winter and on passage	
Black-browed Albatross	Extreme rarity	
Fulmar	Regular	
Manx Shearwater	Scarce	
Leach's Petrel	Very scarce	
Gannet	Regular	
Cormorant	Common	
Shag	Regular	
Bittern	Scarce breeder	
Cattle Egret	Increasingly frequent all year round	
Great (White) Egret	Increasingly frequent all year round	
Grey Heron	Common	
Purple Heron	Very scarce migrant	
White Stork	Scarce migrant: numerous feral birds	
Glossy Ibis	Increasingly frequent all year round	
Spoonbill	Increasingly frequent all year round	
Mute Swan	Common	
Bewick's Swan	Winter resident in some numbers	
Whooper Swan	Winter resident in some numbers	
Taiga Bean Goose	Winter resident in small numbers	
Tundra Bean Goose	Winter resident in small numbers	
Pink-footed Goose	Winter resident in large numbers	
White-fronted Goose	Winter resident in some numbers	
Lesser W-f Goose	Extremely rare winter visitor	
Ross's Goose	All records possibly escapes	

Canada Goose	Common	
Barnacle Goose	Large feral population	
Brent Goose	Winter visitor: uncommon on East Coast	
Egyptian Goose	Common	
Ruddy Shelduck	A few records: most / all are escapes	
Shelduck	Common	
Mandarin	A few seen each year	
Eurasian Wigeon	Winter visitor in large numbers: a few summer	
American Wigeon	Single birds seen almost annually	
Gadwall	Increasingly common resident	
Teal	Winter visitor in large numbers: a few summer	
Green-winged Teal	Rare winter vagrant	
Mallard	Common	
Pintail	Winter visitor in large numbers	
Garganey	Scarce spring migrant	
Shoveler	Abundant throughout year	
Red-crested Pochard	Seen almost annually: most are feral	
Pochard	Increasingly abundant	
Ring-necked Duck	Single birds seen almost annually	
Ferruginous Duck	Very scarce migrant	
Tufted Duck	Abundant throughout year	
Greater Scaup	Occasional winter visitor inland	
Eider	Coastal visitor in winter	
Long-tailed Duck	Coastal visitor in winter	
Common Scoter	Occasional winter visitor inland	
Velvet Scoter	Coastal visitor in winter: occasional inland	
Goldeneye	Occasional winter visitor inland	
Smew	Scarce winter visitor inland	
Red-breasted Merganser	Occasional winter visitor inland	
Goosander	Occasional winter visitor inland	
Ruddy Duck	Formerly bred: following 'cull', very rare visitor	
Honey Buzzard	Very scarce migrant	
Black Kite	Very scarce migrant	

Red Kite	Increasingly frequent resident	
White-tailed Eagle	Vagrant: seen most years	
Marsh Harrier	Increasingly abundant resident	
Hen Harrier	Winter visitor: becoming much less common	
Montagu's Harrier	Rare spring migrant	
Goshawk	Rare: potential breeder	
Sparrowhawk	Fairly abundant resident	
Common Buzzard	Increasingly abundant resident	
Rough-legged Buzzard	Rare winter visitor	
Osprey	Regular passage migrant: could breed soon	
Kestrel	Resident, but becoming less common	
Red-footed Falcon	Annual vagrant	
Merlin	Scarce winter visitor	
Hobby	Fairly abundant summer visitor	
Peregrine	Breeds in small numbers	
Red-legged Partridge	Abundant throughout year	
Grey Partridge	Very scarce in Yare Valley: declining in Norfolk	
Quail	Very rare breeder: formerly more common	
Water Rail	Fairly numerous resident: often heard!	
Spotted Crake	Rare migrant: may occasionally breed	
Corncrake	Extremely rare vagrant	
Moorhen	Abundant throughout year	
Coot	Abundant throughout year	
Little Bustard	One record: bird found shot in 2015	
Oystercatcher	Abundant throughout year	
Avocet	Increasingly abundant throughout year	
Little Ringed Plover	Scarce summer visitor / breeder	
Ringed Plover	Abundant throughout year	
Killdeer	Very rare vagrant	
Caspian Plover	Single old record from Yarmouth	
Dotterel	Rare passage migrant	
American Golden Plover	Very rare vagrant	
Pacific Golden Plover	Very rare vagrant	

European Golden Plover	Present in large coastal flocks in winter	
Grey Plover	Scarce but regular in winter	
Lapwing	Abundant throughout year	
Red Knot	Present in large coastal flocks in winter	
Great Knot	Very rare vagrant	
Sanderling	Fairly common in winter	
Little Stint	Scarce but regular on passage	
Temminck's Stint	Rare passage migrant	
White-rumped Sandpiper	Rare vagrant	
Baird's Sandpiper	Rare vagrant	
Pectoral Sandpiper	Scarce but nearly annual vagrant	
Curlew Sandpiper	Scarce passage migrant	
Purple Sandpiper	Scarce winter visitor to coast	
Dunlin	Present in fairly large numbers in winter	
Broad-billed Sandpiper	Rare passage migrant	
Buff-breasted Sandpiper	Rare vagrant	
Ruff	Fairly common on passage	
Jack Snipe	Fairly widespread but overlooked in winter	
Common Snipe	Abundant throughout year	
Woodcock	Scarce resident and winter migrant	
Black-tailed Godwit	Fairly common on passage	
Bar-tailed Godwit	Fairly common on passage	
Whimbrel	Fairly common on passage	
Curlew	Increasingly scarce resident	
Spotted Redshank	Migrant and scarce winter resident	
Redshank	Abundant throughout year	
Marsh Sandpiper	Rare vagrant	
Greenshank	Regular passage migrant	
Lesser Yellowlegs	Rare vagrant	
Green Sandpiper	Scarce passage migrant	
Wood Sandpiper	Scarce passage migrant	
Common Sandpiper	Migrant and uncommon summer resident	
Turnstone	Abundant throughout year	

Wilson's Phalarope	Rare migrant	
Red-necked Phalarope	Rare migrant	
Grey Phalarope	Rare migrant	
Pomarine Skua	Scarced on passage spring and autumn	
Arctic Skua	Annual on autumn passage	
Long-tailed Skua	Rare on autumn passage	
Great Skua	Annual on autumn passage	
Mediterranean Gull	Increasingly common resident	
Franklin's Gull	Very rare vagrant	
Little Gull	Passage migrant	
Sabine's Gull	Very rare vagrant	
Black-headed Gull	Abundant throughout year	
Ring-billed Gull	Two records: extremely rare vagrant	
Common Gull	Fairly abundant resident and winter visitor	
Lesser Black-backed Gull	Increasingly abundant throughout year	
Great Black-backed Gull	Fairly abundant resident and winter visitor	
Herring Gull	Abundant resident and winter visitor	
Yellow-legged Gull	Scarce vagrant	
Caspian Gull	Scarce vagrant	
Iceland Gull	Scarce winter visitor	
Glaucous Gull	Scarce winter visitor	
Kittiwake	Resident: more numerous in autumn	
Caspian Tern	Scarce vagrant: virtually annual	
Sandwich Tern	Fairly abundant summer visitor	
Roseate Tern	Very scarce passage migrant	
Common Tern	Fairly abundant summer visitor	
Arctic Tern	Scarce on spring passage	
Little Tern	Former breeder: frequent in summer	
Whiskered Tern	Scarce vagrant	
Black Tern	Scarce on spring passage	
White-winged Black Tern	Scarce vagrant	
Guillemot	Fairly common in winter	
Razorbill	Fairly common in winter	

Black Guillemot	Scarce winter visitor	
Little Auk	Scarce on autumn passage	
Puffin	Scarce on autumn passage	
Feral Pigeon	Common resident	
Wood Pigeon	Common resident	
Stock Dove	Resident	
Collared Dove	Abundant resident	
Turtle Dove	Declining breeder: now very scarce	
Ring-necked Parakeet	Still a rare vagrant: increasing	
Cuckoo	Declining breeder: now scarce	
Barn Owl	Widespread resident	
Little Owl	Widespread resident	
Tawny Owl	Widespread resident	
Long-eared Owl	Very scarce passage migrant	
Short-eared Owl	Regular winter visitor	
Common Swift	Summer migrant	
Alpine Swift	Very scarce vagrant	
Kingfisher	Widespread	
Bee-eater	Very scarce vagrant	
Hoopoe	Very scarce vagrant	
Wryneck	Scarce on autumn passage	
Green Woodpecker	Widespread	
Great Spotted Woodpecker	Fairly abundant resident	
Lesser Spotted W/pecker	Probably no longer breeds in Broadland	
Woodlark	Passage migrant	
Skylark	Fairly abundant resident: numbers declining	
Shore Lark	Scarce winter visitor	
Sand Martin	Summer migrant	
Swallow	Summer migrant	
Red-rumped Swallow	Scarce vagrant	
House Martin	Summer migrant	
Richard's Pipit	Scarce vagrant: nearly annual	
Tawny Pipit	Increasingly rare vagrant	

Tree Pipit	Passage migrant	
Meadow Pipit	Abundant resident	
Rock Pipit	Scarce winter visitor	
Water Pipit	Scarce winter visitor	
Yellow Wagtail	Increasingly scarce migrant	
Grey Wagtail	Scarce resident: numbers increasing	
Pied Wagtail	Abundant resident	
White Wagtail	Regular summer visitor	
Bohemian Waxwing	Winter irruptive: virtually annual	
Black-bellied Dipper	Scarce winter visitor	
Wren	Abundant resident	
Dunnock	Abundant resident	
Robin	Abundant resident	
Nightingale	Decreasing summer migrant	
Bluethroat	Rare vagrant	
Red-flanked Bluetail	Very rare vagrant	
Black Redstart	A few breed each year in coastal habitat	
Common Redstart	Regular summer migrant: has bred	
Whinchat	Scarce passage migrant	
Stonechat	Fairly common resident	
Northern Wheatear	Passage migrant: regular	
Desert Wheatear	Very rare vagrant	
Ring Ouzel	Scarce passage migrant	
Blackbird	Abundant resident	
Fieldfare	Abundant winter visitor	
Song Thrush	Declining breeder and passage migrant	
Redwing	Abundant winter visitor	
Mistle Thrush	Resident	
Cetti's Warbler	Increasingly abundant	
Grasshopper Warbler	Annual summer migrant	
Savi's Warbler	Very rare vagrant	
Aquatic Warbler	Exceptionally rare vagrant	
Sedge Warbler	Abundant summer migrant	

Marsh Warbler	Very rare vagrant	
Reed Warbler	Abundant summer visitor	
Booted Warbler	Very rare vagrant	
Barred Warbler	Rare vagrant	
Lesser Whitethroat	Fairly abundant summer visitor	
Common Whitethroat	Abundant summer visitor	
Garden Warbler	Abundant summer visitor	
Blackcap	Abundant summer visitor	
Greenish Warbler	Very rare vagrant	
Pallas' Warbler	Rare vagrant	
Yellow-browed Warbler	Very rare vagrant	
Hume's Warbler	Very rare vagrant	
Radde's Warbler	Very rare vagrant	
Dusky Warbler	Very rare vagrant	
Chiffchaff	Abundant summer visitor	
Siberian Chiffchaff	Very rare vagrant	
Iberian Chiffchaff	Very rare vagrant	
Willow Warbler	Abundant summer visitor	
Goldcrest	Abundant resident	
Firecrest	Scarce migrant and occasional breeder	
Spotted Flycatcher	Increasingly scarce resident	
Red-breasted Flycatcher	Rare migrant	
Pied Flycatcher	Scarce migrant	
Bearded Tit	Scarce resident	
Long-tailed Tit	Abundant resident	
Marsh Tit	Fairly widespread resident	
Willow Tit	May no longer exist in Broadland	
Coal Tit	Fairly abundant resident	
Blue Tit	Abundant resident	
Great Tit	Abundant resident	
Nuthatch	Uncommon resident	
Treecreeper	Fairly widespread resident	

Useful resources

THE following blogs, websites and Twitter feeds are, in my opinion, worth checking before a visit to the Yare Valley: there are also a number of rare bird phonelines whose numbers are available through an internet search.

Birds of Norfolk
http://www.norfolkbirds.com/
Norfolk bird news updated daily, with details of numerous Norfolk birding locations.

Yare Valley Wildlife
http://yarevalleywildlife.synthasite.com/
Maintained by a number of local patchers, the website includes daily records and some photos.

Surfbirds Norfolk bird news 'Tweets'
http://surfbirds.com/ukbirdnews/norfolk.php
Updated throughout the day, news and photos of interesting species and links to local Twitter feeds.

Ben's Birding Blogspot
http://bensbirding.blogspot.co.uk/
Blog of one of the Wardens at Strumpshaw Fen: somewhat irregular posting, but interesting insights to the running of the mid-Yare reserves.

Jim's Birding Blog
http://jimsbirdingblog.blogspot.co.uk/
Jim is a very dedicated patcher and Vol. Asst. Warden at Church Farm Marsh. Useful resource before a planned visit.

James' Birds and Beer
http://jamesbirdsandbeer.blogspot.co.uk/
Maintained by an ultra-dedicated local patcher at Whitlingham Lane, this blog is regularly updated with news of birds, invertebrates, fungi and other interesting wildlife.

Picture credits and thanks

ALL images, including maps, are by the author unless otherwise stated: copy-right is reserved.

As always, thanks to my beautiful and supportive wife Linda: we got together through birdwatching and have shared the passion for over thirty years!

Friends and neighbours Sue and Peter have helped Linda and me maintain our enthusiasm for birds, dining and fine wines, so a real debt of gratitude is owed to them both!

Thanks, too, to good friends Brian and Norman: they have patiently shown me how to take reasonable photographs and put up with my 'bird nerdery' week in and week out. Like Linda, they have given me lots of support and help with the writing of this guide. I am proud to be a member of the infamous 'Last of the Summer Wine' birding crew! Thanks also to honorary LotSWC member Brian Shreeve for the use of four of his fantastic images.

I must also express my gratitude to the 1000 or so people who view my blog every day: you have given me the incentive to write this book and to keep tramping five miles a day around the patch!

Birds of the Heath

http://birdsoftheheath.blogspot.co.uk/

Bibliography

THERE are a number of books that deal with the birdlife of Norfolk, all of which contain references to the Yare Valley. Additionally there are others that, although written some time ago, contain many fascinating anecdotes of the days when bird watching was very much a minority pursuit!

Mark Cocker
'Claxton: Field notes from a small planet' Penguin, 2015

Don Dorling, Michael Seago, Peter Allard & Moss Taylor
'The Birds of Norfolk' , Christopher Helm, 2007

Michael Seago
'Birds of Norfolk' Jarrold, 1966

Neil Glenn
'Best birdwatching sites in Norfolk' Buckingham Press, 2006

Phil Benstead, Steve Rowland & Richard Thomas
'Norfolk: a Birdwatcher's Site Guide' Shoebill Books, 2001

Beryl Tooley
'Scribblings of a Yarmouth Naturalist' B.Tooley, 2004

Richard Millington
'A Twitcher's Diary' Blandford, 1981

Lee G R Evans
'Ultimate Site Guide to Scarcer British Birds' LGRE Productions, 1996

Norfolk & Norwich Naturalists' Society
'The Norfolk Bird and Mammal Report' NNNS Publications, annual

How to take average bird photos!

PEOPLE who know me well accept the fact that I am quite honest with myself: I know what I'm good at and don't mind admitting it! I also know what talents and skills I possess that are just OK: included among these would be painting and drawing, playing the guitar and, I have to be honest, photographing wildlife.

I've taken photos of birds and mammals for well over forty years – I have albums full of fuzzy specks that might be rare birds: these I took with a Praktica 35mm film camera and 300mm lens.

For a number of years Linda and I made and sold rare bird videos around East Anglia (and one on a Scillonian Pelagic) Maybe some of you bought one or two? After a while we grew bored with charging from one end of the county to another to video our fifth Hoopoe of the year, and stopped making them.

A sea-change of sorts occurred when, for one of those 'landmark birthdays', Linda gave me a Pentax K-x DSLR camera and Sigma 70 – 300mm zoom lens. (As all of you probably know, the letters stand for 'digital single lens reflex') The advantage of this piece of kit was immediately obvious to me: I could take hundreds of photos on one SD card and not have to pay lots of money and wait a week for my pictures to come back from Boots (Other high street chemists are available!)

Anecdote: back in the seventies I used several expensive rolls of high ASA film to photograph what remains the best comet I've ever seen: it was called Comet West and was a splendid sight in the dawn sky. Although I had a home darkroom, I wanted to make sure that the films were processed by experts, so I took them into the photographic shop in Norwich (now closed down!) where I had bought the filmstock.

Went I went back to pick them up, the owner plonked four brand new films on the counter, saying "I think that must've been a faulty batch: all 144 negatives just had a blurry streak across the middle." True story!

The gift of the Pentax coincided with my doctor telling me I was a fat b*stard and was in danger of heart attacks and Type 2 diabetes: Linda's cunning plan was to encourage me to take the camera out for a walk every day and thereby lose some weight. To cut a long story short, I walk five miles every day and have done so for six years. I lost 30 kilos (64 pounds in old money!) and, at the time of writing, the combination of diet and exercise seems to be keeping the Type 2 under control.

So what's this got to do with bird photography? Well, instead of sitting in the car and driving to Cley, Titchwell or somewhere even further, my daily walks were around my local patch in the mid-Yare Valley: since then I probably visit Strumpshaw, Buckenham, Cantley and Breydon twice a week!

At the Fen I met three amazingly gifted photographers: Brian Tubby, Norman Tottle and Mark Ollett. At the time I'd just started my **Birds of the Heath** blog, and they gave me links to their Flickr sites to put on it. Needless to say, I couldn't believe the quality of their images: even better than those Linda and I used to buy at twitches in the 'good old days'.

I know size isn't everything, but I remember being amazed at how big – and expensive – some of their lenses were. I also noticed that they all had Nikon cameras. They were kind enough to include me in their regular meetings at the Fen and, over the years Brian and Norman have become regular companions and good friends on days out all over Norfolk and Suffolk. As we walk around together, they give me advice (which has to be repeated ten times for it to stick!) on how to set up the camera for whatever the ambient conditions are. I like to feel I pay them back with fieldcraft and i/d skills. Perhaps!

Anyhow: the following is the quintessence of what I have learned from the guys: a Guide to Bird Photography for non-photographers!

Birds move!

Not a startling revelation, but always important to keep in mind! Since small birds like warblers and tits have the annoying propensity for flitting rapidly around the canopy, the first rule is:

Use the fastest shutter speed you can get away with

Unless you're photographing a piece of taxidermy or something big and sleepy, this could be 1/500 of a second on a hazy day and 1/2000 when it's bright and sunny.

In the 'good old days' there was a thing called 'The Sunny Sixteen Rule', which advised us:

If it's a sunny day, and your aperture is set to F/16 and your ISO to 200, to expose your image correctly, the shutter speed needs to be set to 1/200 (the reciprocal of the ISO number)

Of course modern cameras allow a far greater range of ISO settings: my Pentax KS2, for example, has a top ISO sensitivity of 51,200! Bearing this in mind, we move on to rule number two:

Use the lowest appropriate ISO setting

Look: I'm definitely not an expert, but I discovered quite quickly that high ISOs give a grainy result when you crop or zoom in with your image handling software (I use Irfanview and Paintshop Pro) ISO is, as I mentioned above, a measure of sensitivity: the higher the ISO, the less light needed to produce an image. With an ISO setting of 51,200, I can take pictures in a pitch dark forest! Obviously, then, there is a balance to be achieved here between ISO and shutter speed: you really want a high enough shutter speed with the lowest possible ISO to achieve a sharp non-grainy image. Sometimes you have to bite the bullet and accept that you won't be able to crop in without producing a grainy effect: recently, for example, I was photographing Badgers from a hide at night and use of flash was a definite no-no.: I used an ISO of 6400 and fiddled about with the shutter speed and f-stop settings until I managed some acceptable 'record shots'.

Which leads us on to:

A high f-stop setting gives a greater depth of field
A low f-stop setting gives a wider aperture

OK: this is a lot simpler than it's made out to be in most of the books! Again, though, it's a compromise:

If you have a flock of, say, Bramblings on the grass in front of you, a greater depth of field (**high** f-stop) will mean more are in focus.

On a dull day, a **low** f-stop setting will give you the possibility of a lower ISO or faster shutter speed (Both good things!)

Modern DSLRs have a mind-boggling amount of options on their menus and settings screens: if you want to understand them all, you really do need to read the manual that came with it! (Mine is about an inch thick!)

In general, though, to get started, I'd recommend setting the camera to Aperture Priority (Av or A, depending on the make!), adjusting the f-stop and ISO as appropriate. Here's my next rule:

Take lots of photos, checking as you go

In front of you is a Sandhill Crane: you raise your camera and fill a 16GB SD card. A dog walker flushes it and it flies off, never to be seen again. When you get home, you discover that your camera was set up to photograph last night's delightful sunset, so all the Crane pictures are hopelessly over-exposed. If you check on the rear screen every four or five shots, you can make adjustments and possibly end up with something half-decent!

And lastly:

Big isn't always best

Huge lenses *look* good, but there's really no substitute for being close to something! Heat haze and mist will spoil your images regardless of how big your lens. Fieldcraft is everything: stay quiet, stay still and wait for the bird to come nearer! A 300mm prime lens (ie not a zoom!) with a 1.4 or 1.7 converter will give fabulous results with a decent camera at ranges up to thirty or forty metres and save you ten grand!

Here's the gear I currently use: my default outfit is the K3 with the 300mm prime: absolutely fantastic definition and ease of use! For longer range on brighter days, I use the 150 – 500mm zoom. In the field I always use TrevorHannant stay on protective sleeves!